Presented To

Stacy

On

April 16, 2006

By

Full Gospel Pentecostal Assm
Antigonish, NS
With love!

LIFE ON PURPOSE™ DEVOTIONAL FOR GRADUATES

Real Faith and Divine Direction for Every Day

By

Harrison House

Harrison House
Tulsa, OK

Manuscript written and compiled by Susan Janos, Tulsa, Oklahoma.

09 08 07 06 05   10 9 8 7 6 5 4 3 2 1

Life on Purpose for Graduates:
Real Faith and Divine Direction for Every Day
ISBN 1-57794-727-4
Copyright © 2005 by Harrison House

Published by Harrison House, Inc.
P.O. Box 35035
Tulsa, Oklahoma 74153

Contents

Introduction

When you grasp even a measure of the depth of God's thoughts toward you, there is a lasting change that puts you on course to fulfill your greatest desires and achieve your dreams. He has set your life and purpose in motion before the foundations of the world. He is constantly pushing you toward your destiny. His desire is for you to live and enjoy your life. This book was designed to show you some of the hundreds of ways that the Father God leads and communicates with His children. By learning His ways and His voice, you will be able to leap miles ahead in your destiny and your relationship with God. Each devotional is written from true accounts of people who have been led by God and learned to follow His voice. You will be inspired and amazed at the things God has done. You'll also have an idea of what to expect in your own life with God. You'll discover that it's not so unusual to have great favor, miraculous testimonies, and lasting success when you live your *Life on Purpose.*

No Limits

ELIZABETH

> *Great is our Lord and mighty in power;*
> *his understanding has no limit.*
>
> PSALM 147:5 NIV

I had just moved to a new city and was looking for a job. I had interviewed at several places and was hoping for one job in particular. I was staying with a friend at the time and she was going to be married in one month. She let me know graciously that I needed to have my own place before her wedding day. I felt a tremendous amount of pressure to land a job and money was running short. I was reading my Bible and staying before the Lord, but I felt like nothing was happening.

That week one of my favorite ministers was going to be in town for some special meetings. I thought to myself, *I'm going to go and see if he will pray for me. I know I'll get some kind of direction from God.* The day of the meeting I met my friend for lunch at the hospital where she worked. After lunch, I was walking down the hall to leave the building. I was thinking, *Lord, I am really struggling here and I don't understand why You aren't helping me.* Just then an elderly man came up to me and said, "Why are you so sad? Don't you know that God is taking care of you?" I was shocked! I had never seen this man before in my life. He was a little bit scruffy and holding a pipe. He began to tell me story after story from the Bible of God helping and delivering people. He spoke for an entire hour. I didn't say one word. I stood in that hospital hallway weeping. God was speaking directly to me through an old man that I did not know. When he was finished, I thanked him and he teetered off. I walked to my car completely amazed. God spoke to my heart and said, *You don't need a well-known minister to tell you what to do. I'm taking care of you.* I never did make it to that minister's meeting, and one week later I was hired for the job that I really wanted.

LIVE ON PURPOSE

There are times when God uses supernatural experiences to get through to you. When He moves in these unusual ways, you know it is God by His presence. His peace comes to wash over you. You can read story after story of God's supernatural ways in the Scriptures. He's the same today. Open your heart to God to move in whatever way He wants in your life. Don't limit Him. When the pressures of life seem to mount up, remember that God always has a plan, and part of that plan is for you to trust Him.

PRAYER

Lord, I do not want to limit You. However You want to move in my life is fine with me. I welcome Your plan and Your ways, in Jesus' name.

A New Season

ALYSSA

> *To everything there is a season, A time for every purpose*
> *under heaven…A time to weep, And a time to laugh;*
> *A time to mourn, And a time to dance.*
>
> ECCLESIASTES 3:1,4 NKJV

New pastors, Jade and Christy. I liked them. They were young and fun, but I'd had lots of pastors over the years. Once you'd open up and let them in, they'd move on, never to be heard of again. I'd like to be friends with them. I'd like to be close to them, but if I'd end up being just another face in their past, I'll pass.

Jade and Christy—they won me over. I opened up. I let them in. We had a blast! We partied, learned about God, ministered to others, went on missions trips, and prayed until the compassion of Jesus rose up within us. Then the news came. They were offered another position in another state. But they had become such a big part of my life! When I cried out to God, He took me to Ecclesiastes 3: to everything there is a season, a time for every purpose under heaven. I had Jade and Christy for a season, and now that season was over. I love them, but now I know it's okay that they're leaving. I've been blessed, and it's time to open my heart for new relationships and the seasons God has for me.

LIVE ON PURPOSE

It has been said that there is one thing you can count on in this world, and that one thing is that things will change. We do live in a temporary world, but our stability is found in Jesus. In Hebrews 13 we find that Jesus is the same yesterday, today, and forever. He is forever faithful. When circumstances begin to change around you, you can find yourself unusually stressed and frustrated. You may even feel like giving up. That's when you know it's time to get into God's presence. Turn on the praise and worship music, go to extra church services, and spend time in your own private time with God. Separate yourself from the world for a time until you get your "spiritual feet" again.

PRAYER

*Father God, when things are changing around me,
I ask You to keep me stable. Help me to stay
encouraged and to see the good in every circumstance.
Speak to me through Your Word and let the
peace of God rule in my heart, in Jesus' name.*

Obedient Anyway

CLIFFORD

Trust in the Lord with all your heart,
And lean not on your own understanding;
In all your ways acknowledge Him,
And He shall direct your paths.

PROVERBS 3:5,6

I recently graduated from a Christian college and I was preparing to return for graduate school. As a grad student I had some new options available to me. Finally, I was going to live off campus and not be bound by the restrictive measures of curfew. I'd have my own place, with my own kitchen so I could cook my own food. Forget the cafeteria. And I could invite over anybody I wanted. Sure, I'd have to work a decent job to pay rent while simultaneously taking 12 hours of grad school, but if I lived close to campus, this was doable.

Then amidst an already turbulent summer where God had been dealing with me on a number of issues, I heard

Him speak as clear as day: *I want you to return to campus this next year.* "What's that, God? You want me in an apartment?!" But I knew what He said, and the more I fought His direction, the more uncomfortable I felt.

Nevertheless, I chose the path of obedience and I remained on campus. In less than two weeks into school, I found myself approached with a job promotion. With this promotion I was given $5,000 extra in scholarship, my own fully loaded apartment, and staff privileges exempting me from curfew! God is so good. If I had done things my way I would've stressed myself out with a full-time job and 12 hours of grad school, but God had a much better plan in mind. I'm glad I was obedient!

LIVE ON PURPOSE

God had a much better plan than Clifford did.
His faith in God caused him to choose God's
path even though it did not make sense to him.
Part of trusting God is learning to be obedient
even when we don't understand why. Then
when we look back, we praise God for setting
us up to receive good things. God rewards
those who diligently seek Him. (Heb. 11:6.)

PRAYER

Lord, I repent for not always following Your direction.
I want to trust You with every area of my life.
Help me to keep my body under just like Paul said in
1 Corinthians 9:27. I want my spirit to rule in
my daily and my major decisions, in Jesus' name.

Desires

BRITTANY

> *In his heart a man plans his course,*
> *but the Lord determines his steps.*
>
> PROVERBS 16:9

Graduation came and went. Have diploma. In the real world. Don't know what to do next. Sure, I had plans before college, big plans—go straight to work for a large company, work my way up to CEO, and be a senator. But, something happened while I was in college that changed my perspective.

During my junior year I was alone in my dorm room, and I heard the Holy Spirit speak to me. *You have not completely surrendered your life to Me; you are still holding on to your plans. My plans are far greater than yours.* That realization hit me, and I made a decision that day to totally surrender my life to God. I was now living for His will and purpose. This decision changed me from self-reliant and striving to dependent and knowing.

So, after college I didn't clearly hear from God what to do next, so I started applying for positions, trusting God that He would place me where I needed to be. It wasn't too long until God provided me with a career that I absolutely love. Years from now I don't know where I'll be, but I am confident and full of peace knowing that I am walking in the light of His will!

LIVE ON PURPOSE

Usually God's call on your life is already a strong desire in your heart, but it can take time to discover exactly what that desire is and time for that desire to mature. Psalm 92:13 says that when you are planted in the house of the Lord, you will flourish. When you are committed to the Lord in a local church, it causes you to flourish. And when you are planted where God leads you, you will flourish. Don't be discouraged if you are not where you hoped you would be by now. Check in with God, and if you are where He wants you, that's what matters the most. The rest will come, and He knows when you are ready.

PRAYER

*Father God, I trust You that You have a perfect plan
for me and that it is the best plan. Am I where I should
be right now? Am I doing what You want me to do?
Lord, please show me if I need to make changes or if I need
to just stay put. I am open to Your leading, in Jesus' name.*

Step of Faith

JAYNE

> *Now Faith is the assurance (the confirmation, the title deed) of the things [we] hope for, being the proof of things [we] do not see and the conviction of their reality [faith perceiving as real fact what is not revealed to the senses].*
>
> HEBREWS 11:1 AMP

While employed at a ministry, I began to sense in my spirit a change coming. I told my boss I felt it was time for me to move on. He was a man of God and encouraged me to follow the leading of the Lord. I sent out several applications, but as I continued to seek the Lord on the move, I heard as clearly as if it were an audible voice, *I have given you the desires of your heart and you are to stay here.* I was a bit surprised because I had on the inside to move. I went back to my boss and told him I had heard clearly I was to stay and help him with his vision. He was pleased and agreed it was not the time.

Almost a year later, I received an e-mail from my former secretary at my previous job. "Had I given any thoughts about moving south again?" When I read that, on the inside I felt a wave of excitement. I could not shake it. I e-mailed back and said yes! That e-mail started an amazing chain of events.

I interviewed with a wonderful company. I was hired in a dream-come-true position that would utilize my experience and education. I would be moving to a new state and I needed to sell my home. In two weeks, I sold my home and found an apartment in my new location. I definitely knew it was the right timing and I was in the perfect will of God. Then the tests began. The day before the movers were coming I received a call from my new employer saying the position I was hired for had been eliminated! I was totally caught off guard. My former position was filled, my house was sold, I had movers on the way, and now I had no job. It was a time to reaffirm I had heard from God. When I went to the Lord about it, I felt He told me I was to move. So I packed my car and hit the road for my new city a thousand miles away.

During my drive I listened to teaching and music tapes and continued to have the assurance on the inside I had heard from God. However, my head had some other thoughts. There were more difficulties when I arrived. The movers were delayed so I had no bed, the phone was not hooked up, and things seemed to get worse. I talked with my friends in the Lord and they continued to encourage me that I heard from God and to trust Him.

Well, I had heard from God. Shortly after my arrival, I got a call from the same company who fired me before I even started and they hired me again! I am in the perfect will of God for my life. I am in my "promised land" for this season in my life, and I work with the greatest team of people.

LIVE ON PURPOSE

Hebrews 11:1 in the Amplified version says that faith is the title deed, or confirmation, of things that you cannot see. Your faith gives you the assurance that what you hoped for belongs to you. Once Jayne heard from God to move, it was not all smooth sailing. When doubts arose, she checked back in with God and got counsel from a few of her friends in the Lord. Her faith remained firm, and even though she did not have the job in the natural realm, she had it by faith in the spiritual realm. What have you had your faith out for? Keep it before the Lord and stay strong in faith even if your natural circumstances are not lining up yet.

PRAYER

Father God, I walk by faith and live by faith. Even if I don't see with my natural eyes what You promised me, I will stay strong in faith until I see it come to pass, in Jesus' name.

Faith To Win

JOSHUA

{
Every child of God can defeat the world, and our faith is
what gives us this victory. No one can defeat the world
without having faith in Jesus as the Son of God.
}

1 JOHN 5:4,5 CEV

It was the final event at the track and field competition, the 4 x 400 meter relay. I was going to be our team's anchor leg, which meant I was going to be the final person to run around the track and finish for our team. I was very nervous with this overwhelming task in front of me because we were going up against eight of the very best relay teams in the region, some of which had beaten us badly a couple of weeks prior. I entered the relay area with my team, unsure of my ability to help us finish strongly.

Right before it was my turn to get the baton, I heard God's voice inside say, *When I tell you to sprint, run harder than ever before and you'll fly like an eagle.* I was now even more nervous because I wasn't exactly quite sure when His voice was going to say, *Sprint,* and ask me to run harder than I had ever run before; and I wasn't sure if I was exactly up to this task. I got the baton in last place and took off running, and with about 275 meters left to run in the race I heard "sprint" inside, and I knew it was time for me to go. I had never run with more might than I did once that word jolted through my being. I ended up passing seven runners and winning the relay race for our team, which was our first victory of the season. I know now that when God asks me to do something, I'll obey it because He always has our best in mind and our victory in hand.

LIVE ON PURPOSE

God was concerned about Joshua's race and had a
plan to help him win. Even in your everyday
activities, God is ready to help you. Joshua
recognized God's voice and had faith to obey it.
As you continue to develop your own relationship
with God, you'll begin to recognize His leading
more and more often and have faith in what He
says. He always has your victory in mind.

PRAYER

Father, help me to recognize Your voice—to be able to discern between my own ideas, the enemy, and Your voice. Help me to be diligent to study Your Word and to talk to You. Teach me to follow Your leading in every part of my life and to have faith in what You tell me, in Jesus' name.

My Defender

LIZZY

{
The Lord executes righteousness and justice
[not for me only, but] for all who are oppressed.

PSALM 103:6 AMP
}

I'd been working at a job for about a month when my boss discovered that I was a dedicated Christian. I really had not made a spectacle of myself; I was just living right. He proceeded to harass me at every opportunity. He would joke around and make fun of my church and my beliefs while the other employees were around. I spent a great deal of time in prayer about this. At the same time God gave me great favor with customers, and I landed several big accounts that others had not been able to break into.

One morning my boss called me into his office. His instructions quickly turned to making fun of my faith. He stood up from his desk to emphasize his point, when all of the sudden his chair flew out from under him! With arms scrambling, he tried to catch himself to no avail. He sprawled flat out on the floor. I watched as if it were in slow motion. I quickly asked if he was all right as he rose up from the floor with a red face and a scowl of embarrassment. He told me he was through and I could leave. I don't know if God had something to do with that, but I do know that the Scriptures say in Psalm 103 that He is the defender of those who belong to Him.

I worked there for a few more months, but eventually I felt the Lord release me from that job. On my last day there, the boss called me into his office again. He asked many questions about God with sincerity. I answered and said I would pray for him. I don't know if he ever made a commitment to God, but I do know that I sowed many seeds. Many things I learned from that job prepared me for my next job, which was for a great company. God turned it all for good.

LIVE ON PURPOSE

You may be struggling with where you are
right now, even though you know it's where
God wants you to be. But if you are patient,
God has a way of turning everything around
for good. Remember that God is your defender.
If you bring things before the Lord in prayer,
He will move on your behalf. You don't have
to always stand up for yourself; you can relax
and let God fight your battles for you.

PRAYER

Father God, thank You that You are my defender,
that You execute righteousness and justice for me.
Give me wisdom when I am dealing with people, especially
those who are over me. I want to respect them, but I don't
want to be walked on. Show me what I should say and do
when faced with adverse situations, in Jesus' name.

Stay Open

JULIE

*"My thoughts are completely different from yours," says
the Lord. "And my ways are far beyond anything you
could imagine. For just as the heavens are higher than
the earth, so are my ways higher than your ways
and my thoughts higher than your thoughts."*

ISAIAH 55:8,9 NLT

After two and a half years, Scott and I were excited to be moving back to our hometown with our young family. However, the house we moved into was quite a bit more expensive than the house we had moved from, so it was certain that I would have to return to work.

One cold December morning, after I saw my husband off to work, one daughter off to school, and the other down for her morning nap, I sat down in front of the crackling fireplace with my yellow highlighter to wade my way through the classified ads looking for a new career. After a long morning of dead-end phone calls, I was beginning to get frustrated. The phone rang and I answered it, hoping it was someone calling to set up an interview, but it was only my uncle who had just called to chat. My uncle was not walking with God and wasn't really open to hearing about the gospel, so I did not expect him to give me any real encouragement. After I explained what I was doing, he suggested that I contact a company I had worked for before we moved away. I was strongly opposed to it; I had been there and done that and I was ready for something new. However, after I hung up the phone, the words just kept coming back to me—the feeling just wouldn't go away. Later that afternoon, I decided to call an old friend who was still employed there just to see how things were going. After we talked for a few minutes and I told her that I was job hunting, she exclaimed that she had just been talking about me that same day because they were looking for someone to fill my old position and had heard that I was back in town. By the end of that week I had been hired and was offered more money than I actually needed to make!

That was nearly four years ago, and today I know deep in my heart that God called me to the position I now hold at the company. I love what I do and I have flexible work hours that allow me to be home for my daughters after school and take care of my family. I have the best of both worlds. It scares me to think where I might be today had I not obeyed what God was telling me to do—and He gave me direction through the most unlikely person.

LIVE ON PURPOSE

God works in ways we do not expect, so stay open. He may give you a miraculous deliverance one time and the next time walk you through your trial by practical means. Isaiah 55 says that God's thoughts are higher than your thoughts and His ways higher than your ways. Ecclesiastes 11 says you cannot understand all the works of God, and 1 Corinthians 1:25 shows that the foolishness of God is wiser than man's wisdom. It really gets down to trusting God, no matter how unusual His ways look. And since He lives within you, when the enemy tries to throw you a counterfeit, the Holy Spirit gives you a check in your spirit that something isn't right.

PRAYER

Father God, in Jesus' name, I am going to stay open to Your ways. I receive Your wisdom over my own ideas. I welcome You to work in my life.

Divine Leading

GARY

> However, I (Jesus) am telling you nothing but the
> truth when I say it is profitable (good, expedient,
> advantageous) for you that I go away. Because if I do not
> go away, the Comforter (Counselor, Helper, Advocate,
> Intercessor, Strengthener, Standby) will not come to you
> [into close fellowship with you]; but if I go away, I will
> send Him to you [to be in close fellowship with you].
>
> JOHN 16:7 AMP

After two and a half years of working a job that I enjoyed, I began to sense that a change was coming. At this time I really had it made. I had just bought a nice home two years earlier that was everything I desired in a home. I was the singles' leader at our church, which allowed me to host fellowship activities and also minister God's Word on a weekly basis. I had a lot of great friends and a wonderful church family. Everything was going great, except I began to have a real dissatisfaction on the inside. I knew in my heart that I needed additional spiritual training. Even as a child I had always sensed a call to ministry. Within a few months I was awakened one night and the Holy Spirit began speaking some things to me. I ended up writing a couple of pages, which again confirmed some things that I already had in my heart. Approximately one year after I first sensed a transition, a prophet and his wife came to our church whom I had never met. He began to prophesy over me, and his wife followed up with a word also. Everything they said confirmed what I already had in my heart. Within four months, I was enrolled in a Bible school in another state and rented my house out, which later sold in less than a year!

LIVE ON PURPOSE

There really is a divine leading of the Spirit. That's why God sent the Holy Spirit. The Amplified version of John 16:7 tells us that He is your Counselor, Helper, Advocate, Intercessor, Strengthener, and Standby, and that Jesus sent Him to be in close fellowship with you. The Holy Spirit woke Gary up and gave him specific instructions. Then the Lord sent others to confirm that what he had heard was indeed God. God wants you to know His will for your life, and He's willing to go to great lengths to communicate with you. Open yourself up to receive His divine direction.

PRAYER

Father God, thank You for sending the Holy Spirit to be my counselor. I welcome His leading in my life. Help me to be sensitive to the many ways in which He speaks to me. I am depending upon the Holy Spirit to show me my next move, in Jesus' name.

Leaving the Comfort Zone

ALYSSA

{
When you pass through the waters, I will be with you; and when you pass through the rivers, they will not sweep over you. When you walk through the fire, you will not be burned....
}

ISAIAH 43:2 NIV

I was about to do a four-month internship with Metro Ministries in Brooklyn, New York. About three days before I was to leave, I just really did not want to go anymore. I didn't want to leave my friends. I didn't want to leave my family, and I didn't want to get out of my comfort zone to go somewhere where I didn't know anyone. For those three days, I cried out to God asking Him why I was doing this. I got to the point where I said, "God, if I don't tangibly hear Your voice on this, I'm not going!" I remember lying there in bed crying. And then God just said, "You need to go to see how blessed you truly are." At the time, I was having problems at home and I really wasn't on the right path with God. I think God wanted me to go to get a reality check. When God spoke to me, I got this peace. It came over me, and I knew that I was going to be fine. And so I did it. I met some amazing people. I did some things I never thought I could or would do! I made some life-long friends. But most of all, because of my obedience to God, my relationship with Christ grew stronger and closer than it ever had been in my life.

LIVE ON PURPOSE

Have you felt God has given you a specific task? Is it outside of your comfort zone? Many times God will call you to go up higher—to come to a new level of commitment to Him. Even though part of you may not want to go forward, the rewards of allowing God to take you to a new level are always tremendous. Search your heart. Is there something that God is asking you to do?

PRAYER

Father God, I submit myself to Your will.
If there is something You want me to do outside
of my comfort zone, help me to have courage and
to move forward toward that goal. When I want
to hesitate, help me to persevere, in Jesus' name.

Transformed

AMY

> *And do not be conformed to this world, but be transformed by the renewing of your mind, that you may prove what is that good and acceptable and perfect will of God.*
>
> ROMANS 12:2 NKJV

I was always a social kid and had lots of friends. During my sophomore year of high school, my dad's job transferred us to another city. I had to start over at the beginning of my junior year in a new school where I knew no one. It was a shock to me that I was not accepted right away. I felt terribly lonely and rejected. There was nothing my parents or I could do to change the situation. In my desperation, I turned to God. I cried out to Him for help and spent time with Him every day seeking His love and His direction for my life. The most amazing thing started to happen. All those feelings of needing to be accepted by others began to disappear. Instead, my confidence began to grow in Christ. I became rooted and grounded in His love, and the love of others became secondary. I did eventually make friends, but I will be forever thankful to the Lord that I was able to find Him.

LIVE ON PURPOSE

The world promotes popularity, and it's easy to get caught up in wearing the right clothes and driving the right car to be accepted. It's really a trap that makes you feel insecure in yourself. But when you discover who you are in Christ, your inner man is strengthened. The pressures of the world cannot crush you into their mold. You begin to experience the freedom that can only be found in Christ Jesus. If you have been struggling with your self-worth, take some time to find out who you are in Christ. Look up all the Scriptures in the New Testament epistles that say "in Him," "in Whom," or "in Christ."

PRAYER

Lord, I do not want to be conformed to this world,
but I want to be transformed by the renewing of my mind.
Help me to understand who I am in Christ Jesus.
Help me to break away from negative influences of
the world that damage my self-worth. Ground me
in Your love and faithfulness, in Jesus' name.

Seek Him

RENOULTE

{ *You will seek me and find me when you seek me with all your heart.* }

JEREMIAH 29:13 NIV

I was driving home from work thinking, *Why am I so unfulfilled?* I had a great job, a house, a beautiful wife, and a child on the way. I had everything I could ever want, yet I was bored. I told God that if this is all that life has to offer, then He should just come back so I could go to heaven. I heard God say to me, *I have a greater plan for your life.* So I began to seek His face like I never had before. Then one day I got the answer. I was supposed to go to Bible school and open up a school for teenagers that teaches them about God, entrepreneurship, and the arts. I sold my house and moved my family halfway across the country to give my life some meaning. It has been an amazing ride. I have never been happier and my family never better now that my life has purpose. I know why God placed me on this earth. I know that I am in His will, and there is no other place I would rather be.

LIVE ON PURPOSE

You could have a relationship with God and a decent life, but it will not compare to God's perfect will in your life. God's best does not come to you on a silver platter. God must be sought out with your whole heart before His best is found. If you have only played around with religion, you may want to rethink that strategy. God is the Almighty and He wants all of you. That's how you get all of Him.

PRAYER

Father God, in Jesus' name, You are first in my life.
I know that nothing can compare to You,
and I want to really know that for myself.
Teach me Your ways and show me Your truth.

God Speaks

MARCINE

But Jesus said, "It is written, 'Man is not to live on bread only. Man is to live by every word that God speaks.'"

MATTHEW 4:4 NLV

I'll never forget that day. I was looking out the north window at my aunt's house. I was daydreaming about nothing when inside I heard, *You'll go to Bible school for three years and then get married.* I just thought, *oh,* and basically blew it off.

The summer after graduation came, and my pastor grabbed me after church and asked me if I wanted to go to Bible school. Immediately I remembered that day I was looking out the window. I looked at my pastor intently and said confidently, "Yes." I knew I was supposed to go. My dad thought I was crazy. There was a university seven miles from where I lived. Why would I want to go out of state to a Bible college? But I stuck to what I knew was right in my spirit. I went three years, met a super guy, and got married. I know God speaks, and He speaks to me.

LIVE ON PURPOSE

God knew you before the foundations of the earth. He planned your existence. The Amplified version of Ephesians 2:10 says, "For we are God's [own] handiwork (His workmanship), recreated in Christ Jesus, [born anew] that we may do those good works which God predestined (planned beforehand) for us [taking paths which He prepared ahead of time], that we should walk in them [living the good life which He prearranged and made ready for us to live]." He has a specific plan for your life. When He speaks to you, take note of it. It may not happen immediately, but when it does, you'll be ready.

PRAYER

Lord, my heart is after You to do those things that
You have already planned for me to do. I'm ready to
follow You. I'm waiting to hear Your direction for my life.
I refuse to make decisions because of circumstances.
I want Your best for my life, in Jesus' name.

An Open Door

ANGEL

I know your deeds. See, I have placed before
you an open door that no one can shut.
I know that you have little strength, yet you have
kept my word and have not denied my name.

REVELATION 3:8 NIV

I did not want to go to a Christian university. I wanted to go to a state university that had ivy growing on the brick buildings and get a Broadcast Journalism degree. That is not how it happened. My adopted grandparents encouraged me to visit a Christian university in the Midwest, which I did. I applied and doors began to open rapidly. I saw the open doors as God's voice saying, *Go ahead*. I was accepted and awarded two scholarships. I had God's peace in my heart concerning the situation. The second semester of my freshman year I was accepted into the Resident Advisor Program and received another scholarship. I not only graduated with a Broadcast Journalism degree, I now have divine connections with friends and job connections that have taken me all over the world. Most importantly, my life was impacted spiritually. For four years I was able to spend Sunday nights in Campus Church and watch the Lord heal my heart and draw me close to His. I am forever grateful for walking through those open doors.

LIVE ON PURPOSE

God has a way of pushing you toward your destiny. Many times it may not be what you are thinking is going to happen. But God works through people and things to bring you His divine appointments. You will never truly be happy until you realize your divine destiny. You have to trust God. His best is what will make you the happiest. Look for those open doors and receive whatever God has.

PRAYER

Lord, I don't want to deceive myself. Your Word says that I have the mind of Christ. You give me perfect knowledge of every situation when I need it. I trust You to bring me into the destiny that will satisfy my soul and allow me to be a blessing to Your Kingdom, in Jesus' name.

Lost and Found

ABRAHAM

> *For the Son of man is come to seek
> and to save that which was lost.*
>
> LUKE 19:10 KJV

I grew up in Bangladesh. My family and I were Muslims, and I learned the Koran like all good Muslims do. I was very diligent to follow the teachings of Mohammad because I desperately wanted to please Allah. The punishments in the Koran are harsh and I was driven by fear. One of my duties was to ring the bells in the mosque when it was time for prayers. I never missed my duty. But no matter what I did, I still felt that I was going to perish because I was not pleasing Allah. One night after evening prayers I stayed in the mosque and prayed all night to Allah. I was hoping I would hear or feel something from him, but nothing happened. As morning approached, I felt something drip on my hand. I looked around but saw nothing. It was an oily substance. It began to fall over my whole body. It only fell on me, not on the floor around me. An amazing presence washed over me. I did not know what it meant, but I knew something supernatural happened to me. Several months later in another supernatural experience I heard an audible voice say to me, *Read the Bible.* No one was around and the voice was very clear, but I could not find a Bible in Bangladesh. Several years later I was sent to the United States as a missionary for Islam. I found a Bible while visiting a library and it was written in Bangladesh! The librarian noticed that I was reading it and asked if I would like to keep it. I gratefully accepted it. As I read about Jesus, I began to have many questions. As I was walking through the park one day, I ran into a professor that I knew. I was aware that he was a Christian. I began to ask him many questions. He answered them all and asked me if I would like to accept Jesus. I knew if I did my family would disinherit me and my friends would abandon me. I thought carefully and decided that I did not want to serve Allah who was so harsh and listen to Mohammad who was dead. Rather I wanted to serve the living God who loved me so much He gave His life for me. I accepted Jesus that day. I lost my family and my friends, but Jesus guarded me and brought me to a safe place. I attended Bible school and eventually received my doctorate. God gave me a beautiful wife, and her family is my family.

LIVE ON PURPOSE

Jesus loves people. His heart is to reach them wherever they are. If you have not accepted Jesus to be your Lord, or if you have been away from Him, then Jesus is seeking you. Make Jesus your Lord now by praying the salvation prayer at the back of this book. If you are already born again, Jesus left you a great commission in Matthew 28. His command is to teach all nations about Him. Short-term mission trips are excellent for ministering to others. Check out www.teenmania.com or www.victorytulsa.org for more information. You can also get involved in your local church. "Missions" is not only going to another country. There are many people who need to hear the gospel in your own nation.

PRAYER

Lord, I want to reach others for You. Show me if I should get involved with a missions team, and help me to be a witness for You here in my own nation, in Jesus' name.

Fear of Failure

DEVON

> *Fear not [there is nothing to fear], for I am with you; do*
> *not look around you in terror and be dismayed, for I am*
> *your God. I will strengthen and harden you to difficulties,*
> *yes, I will help you; yes, I will hold you up and retain you*
> *with My [victorious] right hand of rightness and justice.*
>
> ISAIAH 41:10 AMP

I graduated from Bible college with aspirations of being some big name youth pastor. Very shortly into that ministry I was greeted by frustration and trouble. It was not long afterwards I found myself really questioning God's call on my life. As I prayed I wanted an out; I rationalized that the public school system was a tremendous ministry field. I set off for college, again, and became a certified elementary teacher. As I contemplated where the Lord would have me teach, I determined that an urban public school was where I should go. After all, 70 percent of African-Americans are fatherless, and a male teacher could make quite an impact on their lives. For the next two and a half years I was miserable. The students needed structure, tough love, and firm boundaries. I was more relational, unstructured, and little more of a pushover. The contrast made for a couple of challenging years. I was trying to do a good thing but not what God had purposed for me because of a fear of failing. During this time we had a new pastor at our church; he believed in me and encouraged me to pursue leadership in the church. His encouragement helped me step up into the leadership ministry again where I had felt so hurt before.

I knew then I would no longer teach at the year's end. During a Steven Curtis Chapman concert, I saw a video biography of five missionaries who went to the Ecuador Indians and were all ultimately speared to death. Then, one of the wives later would go back into that same tribe; many were converted and a church was born. Chapman came back on the stage and introduced one of the children of the original missionaries and one of the tribes-men who helped kill those missionaries but was now serving God. I was so moved by God's grace and mercy that I was a weeping faucet by that time. It was as if I could see those missionaries who gave their lives looking over and saying, "It was all worth it." In that moment God minis-tered to me. I realized I had been living to do good for God, but not His best that He had for me. I was living with a fear of failure rather than trusting that God would provide and equip me. It was there I determined to obey what God had called me to do a long time before. I pastor a church now and know that I'm doing what God called me to do.

LIVE ON PURPOSE

When God calls you, He equips you as well. He is not limited by your education, background, family, or past failures. He's gifted you with specific talents because He is good and His gifts are forever. Determine to trust God to complete your calling and purpose in the earth.

PRAYER

Father God, I trust You to help me complete Your purpose for my life. I refuse to fear failure or any other thing. Thank You for strengthening me and hardening me to difficulties so that I can do what You called me to do, in Jesus' name.

The One

{ *Then you will not become spiritually dull and indifferent. Instead, you will follow the example of those who are going to inherit God's promises because of their faith and patience.* }

HEBREWS 6:12 NLT

The first day Tami came to work, I was immediately attracted to her. I felt impressed one day to have lunch in the work lunchroom. She happened to be there having lunch. We ended up talking together the entire lunch hour. Over time, I asked her out three different times, but she had something else going on each time. The fourth time I called her, I asked her way in advance. It intrigued her enough to say yes. On the third date, I knew in my heart she was the one. As I got ready for work that morning, I was thinking of her. I was looking in the mirror when God spoke to me and said, *Be patient and wait, for this is important to you.* I'd drive over and scrape the ice off of her windows, start her car to warm it up, bring her flowers every month—whatever I could do to show her how I felt. We dated for some time and talked about getting married. Before Valentine's Day that year I could not get a hold of her. That Monday she broke up with me.

I knew in my heart the word I heard that day looking in my mirror was from the Lord. Tami was the one. So I waited. We still worked in the same company and I would see her often. Frustrated, I talked to my friend Andrell about Tami. I asked her, "How do you hold on to someone but let go at the same time?" She reminded me of the story of Abraham and Isaac. Abraham got all the way to the altar to sacrifice his son, but it was not until the very end that God stopped him and provided another sacrifice. I had to hold on to the word God gave me, but let go of that relationship and trust God to bring it back. Several months went by. We started talking again just casually. Then one day something happened in Tami. I could tell in her eyes that her heart had changed and that she was in love with me. She gave me many signs that she wanted me to ask her out again, but I felt like she needed to make the first move. One night she called and asked if we could meet. Through the course of the meeting, she told me that she loved me. I asked her if she understood what that meant. I was committed to being married to her and spending the rest of my life with her. She said yes! Almost a year after

she broke up with me, we were married—February 5th the
following year.

LIVE ON PURPOSE

The word God gave Kyle did not really make sense
until Tami broke up with him. But when that time
came, Kyle had something definite from God to
hold on to. Kyle's faith and patience helped him to
receive the promise he knew was from God.
Patience is a force that will help you persevere in
faith and receive the good things God has for you.
Whatever you are believing God for today,
determine to set your heart on God's promises,
and allow faith and patience to strengthen you.

PRAYER

*Lord, I know patience is a force that will help me
persevere in faith. Give me peace to be patient
and help me to be strong in faith so that I
can receive Your promises, in Jesus' name.*

Led by the Spirit

BARNABAS AND PAUL

In the church at Antioch there were prophets and
teachers: Barnabas, Simeon called Niger, Lucius of Cyrene,
Manaen (who had been brought up with Herod the
tetrarch) and Saul. While they were worshiping the Lord
and fasting, the Holy Spirit said, "Set apart for me
Barnabas and Saul for the work to which I have called
them." So after they had fasted and prayed, they placed
their hands on them and sent them off.

The two of them, sent on their way by the Holy
Spirit, went down to Seleucia and sailed from there to
Cyprus. When they arrived at Salamis, they proclaimed
the word of God in the Jewish synagogues. John was with
them as their helper.

They traveled through the whole island until they
came to Paphos. There they met a Jewish sorcerer and false
prophet named BarJesus, who was an attendant of the
proconsul, Sergius Paulus. The proconsul, an intelligent
man, sent for Barnabas and Saul because he wanted to

hear the word of God. But Elymas the sorcerer (for that is what his name means) opposed them and tried to turn the proconsul from the faith. Then Saul, who was also called Paul, filled with the Holy Spirit, looked straight at Elymas and said, "You are a child of the devil and an enemy of everything that is right! You are full of all kinds of deceit and trickery. Will you never stop perverting the right ways of the Lord? Now the hand of the Lord is against you. You are going to be blind, and for a time you will be unable to see the light of the sun."

Immediately mist and darkness came over him, and he groped about, seeking someone to lead him by the hand. When the proconsul saw what had happened, he believed, for he was amazed at the teaching about the Lord.

ACTS 13:1-12 NIV

LIVE ON PURPOSE

In the book of Acts, Paul and the early
believers depended on the leading of the Holy
Spirit. When they needed direction, they fasted
and prayed until they got it. And the results
were supernatural. Fasting isn't always
appealing, but it changes you like nothing else
can. It gives your inner man the lead position
instead of your flesh. If you need direction
from God, you may want to fast a couple of
meals and spend some time in prayer.

PRAYER

*Father God, I want You to lead me when I should fast
and pray. During those times, help me to keep my
body under and stay focused on You, in Jesus' name.*

The Way of Wisdom

> *I (God) guide you in the way of wisdom and lead you
> along straight paths. When you walk, your steps will
> not be hampered; when you run, you will not stumble.*
>
> PROVERBS 4:11,12 NIV

Bible school had come to an end. Now what? I was trained and ready to go...or so I thought. It was decision-making time again, a place which histori-cally has been difficult for me.

I decided to visit my hometown and just trust the Lord to show me the way. One morning I woke up hearing God tell me exactly where to apply for a job. Could this really be the right direction? Where was this place located, and are they even hiring? There was only one way to find out.

I submitted my application with very little knowledge of the situation, except those words from the Lord. I did so knowing that this would mean relocating...again. I just wasn't finding employment where I had attended school. So, I decided to move regardless of whether this job came through or not. I knew what my spirit was telling me.

Within a few days of arriving in this new town, I had an interview at the place that God had instructed me to apply and was hired on the spot. After months of looking for employment, it became clear that I had been looking in the wrong place! His provision was there all along—only in the place of His wisdom and not mine.

LIVE ON PURPOSE

Isaiah 55 says God's ways are higher than your ways and that His thoughts are not your thoughts. But the good news is that since Jesus came to redeem humanity, God has made a way to impart His thoughts and ways to you. In Ephesians it says that we have the mind of Christ. When you get alone with God through the Word and in prayer, God is able to reveal His wisdom to you. Take some time to find out what God has in store for you today.

PRAYER

*Father God, thank You that because of
Jesus' sacrifice there is a way for You and
I to communicate. I want to know what You have
for me today. Help me to walk in Your wisdom
and not my own human wisdom, in Jesus' name.*

Trust God

CHRISTOPHER

> *Trust in the Lord with all your heart, And lean not on your own understanding; In all your ways acknowledge Him, And He shall direct your paths.*
>
> PROVERBS 3:5,6 KJV

I had just got out of the Air Force and come home for a while before I decided on what to do next. The singles group at my church was having a Hawaiian luau, but I really did not want to go. My mother encouraged me to go, and after much debate, I gave in. Instead of driving to the store to pick up a dish for the event, I had the intention of just driving around to pass the time. I felt the Spirit of the Lord prompt me to go ahead and go to the luau, but I kept fighting it. I drove into the church parking lot only to drive away twice. The third time I finally parked and went in. Feeling uncomfortable with my surroundings and not knowing a single person, I really wanted to leave and just about did. But then, a beautiful girl walked in and sat down beside me. It was the first time I saw my future wife.

LIVE ON PURPOSE

When you feel uncomfortable with God's direction, you have to push yourself past your own feelings and keep your trust in God. Sometimes it's not easy to disregard what your head is telling you, but when you acknowledge God in all your ways, He is able to put you in the right place at the right time. Proverbs 3:5-6 are great Scriptures to pray over your life every day. Let God give you divinely appointed connections.

PRAYER

Father God, I trust in You with all my heart.
I will not lean on my own understanding, but
in all my ways I will ask for Your direction.
Thank You that You direct my paths, in Jesus' name.

For Freedom

KATE

I consider myself a dancer. Ever since my mother enrolled me in dance classes at the age of three, I haven't been able to stop dancing. When I was in high school, a college student at my church decided to start a worship dance group, and of course my sister and I were thrilled to be involved. I began to learn that I could praise God through dance. I began to use the gift that God had given me to bring others into worship. It became a gift I could present to God in any season of my life, be it joy or sorrow.

When I came to college, I didn't feel that I could worship God with dance like I had at home. I felt that if I ever started dancing during worship that I would be drawing too much attention to myself instead of God. In February of my sophomore year, my grandma sent me a letter with a quote she thought I would like from Martha Graham.

> There is a vitality, a life-force, an energy, a quickening that is translated through you into action, and because there is only one of you in all of time, this expression is unique. And if you block it, it will never exist through any other medium and be lost.

God spoke to me through this quote. He created me to be a dancer, and when I dance for His glory, it pleases Him. Now when I feel His gentle nudge to dance during worship, I'm not afraid. I find a quiet, secluded corner and dance for my King, because if I don't, the moment to praise my God will be lost forever.

LIVE ON PURPOSE

Kate let circumstances hinder her worship
for God. But God was patient to bring her
understanding of His will for her life. God's
desire is for His children to be free. Free to
worship Him in spirit and in truth. Is there
something holding you back—something
stealing your freedom? Take it back.
Live in the truth God has provided you.

PRAYER

*Lord, I want to live in the freedom You provided
for me—in worship, in relationships, in life.
Help me to be courageous and stand against those
things that would try to steal my freedom. Even in my
own mind, help me to overcome any strongholds that
are holding me back from Your best, in Jesus' name.*

Save My Family

DIANA

> *And they said, Believe on the Lord Jesus Christ,*
> *and thou shalt be saved, and thy house.*
>
> ACTS 16:31 KJV

Even as a young child I could feel the presence of God. I knew He was with me and He had a plan for my life. I remember crying out to God for lost souls, especially those of my unsaved family members. The prayer I prayed most as a child was, "God, save my daddy. He needs You, Lord. I'm placing another block on the altar for my dad, Lord." I used to keep a count of how many blocks that I had placed on the altar. As I grew older I lost count, but I kept the same prayer. I had several opportunities to witness to my dad over the years. Each time I remember trembling, knowing I would receive a gruff response to my petition for his salvation, and each time it came. Oftentimes I would walk away shivering and unsettled. But I kept trying.

After twenty years passed, I got the courage to tell my dad about the prayer I'd prayed since I was a little girl. I told him, "Dad, God's going to answer my prayer and knock that altar down." A few years later, I left a book in his truck one day entitled *End-Time Events* by Charles Capps. Two days later he called me and in his gruff voice said, "Diana, did you leave that book in my truck?" I wanted to hide, but I was brave and said, "Yes, Dad." Then something happened; he started to cry. My dad, 6 foot 5, 275 pounds, tough guy, crying. Then he said, "Did you know that God loved me before the foundations of the earth? That if I had been the only person left on this earth he would have died just for me?"

"Yes, Dad," I answered. "Jesus loves you. He has always loved you."

I explained the plan of salvation over the phone, but he could not say the prayer with me. I told him that I loved him and that I was always available if he needed someone to talk or pray with. I hung up the phone and cried out to God. What did I do wrong? The Lord spoke to my heart and reassured me that He was doing a work in my dad. I did not give up but kept praying in earnest for my dad.

In 2004, at the age of 59, my dad accepted the Lord Jesus Christ as his personal Savior. I'm sure God's view is more spectacular now that the block altar a small girl built is now removed from His sight. What was once lost is now found; what was blind now sees. Praise be to God!

LIVE ON PURPOSE

God gave you a promise in the Bible in the book of Acts about your family. You can claim your family's salvation according to Acts 16:31. In Matthew 9:38 Jesus instructed the disciples to pray for laborers to be sent into the harvest of souls. You can pray right now for laborers to be sent to your family to minister the gospel to them. God wants your family to be saved more than you do. Stand on His promises and follow His leading on how to talk to your family.

PRAYER

Father God, in Jesus' name, I'm asking You to send laborers to my unsaved family members to minister the gospel to them in a way that they can receive it. I claim my family for the kingdom of God, according to Acts 16:31.

Money

J U L I E

> *But my God shall supply all your need according*
> *to his riches in glory by Christ Jesus.*
>
> PHILIPPIANS 4:19 KJV

At the beginning of my senior year of high school, I began praying and seeking God for direction in the next phase of my life. I felt deep down inside that Oral Roberts University was where God was calling me to go. However, it was almost 1,000 miles from my small hometown and I would need a miracle financially.

I shared this information with my parents, and we all prayed together that God would provide the way for me. My mom was staying home at the time with my younger brother but felt it necessary to go back to work if I was going to go to ORU. Being a teacher, she felt like she would have to wait until the following school year to go back to work since the school year had already begun. So, we just left it in God's hands to provide the way for me.

One fall morning, my mother was leaving our house to run some errands. When she opened the door, there sat on the porch a small white mug. When she picked it up, it had "Oral Roberts University" across the front in beautiful gold lettering as well as ORU's logo. We took this as confirmation for what God was going to do for me, and we still aren't sure who placed the mug on our porch.

Several weeks later, we got a call that my mom had been offered a teaching job beginning the second semester in January. Our family was thrilled and saw this as God's provision since normally teachers don't quit in the middle of the school year.

God did provide, and I went on to attend ORU that next fall. I've met life-long friends, finished my degree, married a wonderful man, and now we have a new baby. Praise God for His provision.

LIVE ON PURPOSE

You may have a knowing inside about what
you are supposed to do in the future. Even if
it looks impossible, if God wants you to do it,
God will make a way for it to happen. Start
to release your faith by finding Scriptures
about God's provision, pray about them,
and speak them over your future.

PRAYER

Father, I know that You have provision
for me to do what You called me to do.
Thank You that You supply all my needs according
to Your riches in glory by Christ Jesus.

Crucial Decisions

ALICE

> *For though ye have ten thousand instructors*
> *in Christ, yet have ye not many fathers: for in*
> *Christ Jesus I have begotten you through the gospel.*
>
> 1 CORINTHIANS 4:15 KJV

Having grown up in Iowa, I had no idea that someday I'd move farther north to the near arctic temperatures of South Dakota! But I had moved there to be a part of a small church to receive some discipleship that would help me grow in the Lord. After about three years, the pastor suggested that I think about going to Bible College. It was a new thought for me. There was a school in Montana that I had visited, and one of the members of our church was teaching there. Moving there sounded like a good and comfortable idea. However, my pastor and his wife came to me and said that they felt that I should pray about attending Christ For The Nations in Dallas, Texas. I thought, *No way am I going down there all by myself!* But almost immediately I knew in my spirit that it was right. Well, I wrestled with that idea with fear and trembling for a few days. In my heart, I knew Dallas was the right choice. I followed that peace and made the move.

One thing I have learned is that being led by the Spirit of God is key to everything in life. It's not always about what makes sense and what is comfortable; it's about faith in Him and His guidance. That decision changed my life completely, and it was the best school I could have attended. The friends that I have made, and the places I have gone, have all pretty much been related to that one decision. When it comes to crucial decisions for our lives, it is imperative that we follow the plan that God has for us. We'll never go wrong following Him, no matter what the circumstances seem like.

LIVE ON PURPOSE

Even though a certain direction may seem good, make sure you take time to find out if it's God's plan for you. In Proverbs 15:22 it says that plans can fail without advisors and in the multitude of counselors there is success. Bounce your ideas off your spiritual leaders—people you know hear from God and people you trust. Sometimes you may have part of it right, but not the whole picture. Alice was right about going to Bible college, but she was looking in the wrong place. God used her pastors—people she trusted—to help her reevaluate. Ultimately, however, the decision was between her and God.

PRAYER

Lord, give me wisdom for crucial decisions.
Send mentors and wise counselors around me to help me
determine how You are leading me, in Jesus' name.

Disappointments

TRECIE

{ *Direct my footsteps according to your word;*
let no sin rule over me. }

PSALM 119:133 NIV

I didn't make the cheerleading squad. Nursing my sorrows, self-pity, and the cumbersome chip on my shoulder in a jumbo bag of potato chips, I mentally ran down my list of twenty-one questions: "Why, God, why? Why did this have to happen to me? Were my cheers not good enough, loud enough, exuberant enough?" I renounced sins I hadn't even committed and even rebuked the devil for stealing and devouring my fifteen minutes of fame. Suddenly, my father's story arrested my self-destructive train of thought.

"An ant depends on its antennae to map out its surroundings," he said. "When an ant senses that a human finger or foot is nearby, it scurries away and changes direction. God often pushes us toward our destiny even though we cannot see it. Somewhere between His finger and our frenzy, we'll walk right into the place where He wants us to be."

This setback was merely God's divine setup for a comeback. During high school, one of the school's news anchors moved to another state, leaving a vacancy...and an opportunity. I felt the Holy Spirit tell me to try out for the position. I loved to read and write, but I had my reservations. I did not want another rejection. Yet, I surrendered to the Holy Spirit and tried out. Four years and hundreds of stories, weather reports, and interviews later, I found my niche in broadcast journalism.

LIVE ON PURPOSE

In Romans 8 we are promised that God will work all things together for good for those who are the called according to His purpose. The preceding verses speak about prayer. When you experience disappointment, get in prayer about it right away. Allow God to turn those situations for good in your life—to help push you toward your destiny. He has a specific plan for you, and He wants you to discover exactly what that is.

PRAYER

Father, I want You to order my steps according to Your Word and Your plan for my life. Give me wisdom to make good decisions. Help me to be strong even in the face of disappointments. I know You have a plan for me that will satisfy the desires of my heart, in Jesus' name.

No Revenge

LIZZY

> *Beloved, do not avenge yourselves, but rather give place to wrath; for it is written, "Vengeance is Mine, I will repay," says the Lord. Therefore "If your enemy is hungry, feed him; If he is thirsty, give him a drink; For in so doing you will heap coals of fire on his head." Do not be overcome by evil, but overcome evil with good.*
>
> ROMANS 12:19-21 NKJV

God has always stuck up for me, and I've learned to pray and trust in Him instead of myself when things get messy. I was working in a small company where everyone knew everyone else. For some reason, the IT director seemed to be irritable every time I asked for help. I prayed about it and tried to keep my mouth shut. Gossip is so tempting, but I knew it would not help me. On one occasion I asked the IT director a question which upset him greatly. He began to yell at me! Just then the president of the company showed up. He asked if everything was all right. Well, that quieted the IT director. He stumbled over his explanation and the president told him there was no need for yelling. I know God ordered that entire situation. He rescued me and the IT director was much nicer to me after that. In fact, I always treated him with respect and we eventually became friends.

LIVE ON PURPOSE

Don't give any place to revenge, except to let God handle it. When you do, the blessings that come are really fabulous. Lizzy discovered that if she would let the Lord handle her problems, He would do it. She did not need to get angry or yell back; she simply reacted in love and trusted God to rescue her. That's not always easy to do, especially at first. You may have to fight your flesh, but the more you stay focused on God and His Word, the easier it gets. Not only did she hold her tongue, but she treated the person who was mean to her with respect. He did not deserve it, but she did it anyway. Her good won out. Check your own life. Are there people who have not treated you right? Give God something to work with. Let your good overcome their evil ways.

PRAYER

Father God, in Jesus' name, help me trust You
and hold my tongue when people come against me.
Remind me of Your promise to take care of me. I know
Your solution is best for me and the other person as well.

Told by the Spirit

PHILIP

Now an angel of the Lord said to Philip, "Go south to the road—the desert road—that goes down from Jerusalem to Gaza." So he started out, and on his way he met an Ethiopian eunuch, an important official in charge of all the treasury of Candace, queen of the Ethiopians. This man had gone to Jerusalem to worship, and on his way home was sitting in his chariot reading the book of Isaiah the prophet. The Spirit told Philip, "Go to that chariot and stay near it."

Then Philip ran up to the chariot and heard the man reading Isaiah the prophet. "Do you understand what you are reading?" Philip asked.

"How can I," he said, "unless someone explains it to me?" So he invited Philip to come up and sit with him.

The eunuch was reading this passage of Scripture: "He was led like a sheep to the slaughter, and as a lamb before the shearer is silent, so he did not open his mouth. In his humiliation he was deprived of justice.

*Who can speak of his descendants? For his life was
taken from the earth."*

*The eunuch asked Philip, "Tell me, please, who is the
prophet talking about, himself or someone else?" Then
Philip began with that very passage of Scripture and told
him the good news about Jesus. As they traveled along the
road, they came to some water and the eunuch said, "Look,
here is water. Why shouldn't I be baptized?" And he gave
orders to stop the chariot. Then both Philip and the eunuch
went down into the water and Philip baptized him. When
they came up out of the water, the Spirit of the Lord
suddenly took Philip away, and the eunuch did not see him
again, but went on his way rejoicing. Philip, however,
appeared at Azotus and traveled about, preaching the
gospel in all the towns until he reached Caesarea.*

ACTS 8:26-40 NIV

LIVE ON PURPOSE

Philip was told by the Spirit what to do. The
Holy Spirit may have spoken in an audible
voice or only to Philip in his inner man.
Philip's experience is evidence of how the
Holy Spirit leads today. It's not unusual for
God to speak to you on a regular basis. After
Philip led the Ethiopian to Jesus, Philip
disappeared and showed up in another city!
Real adventure is knowing and serving God.

PRAYER

*Father God, in Jesus' name, my desire is
to be led by You just as You led Philip.
Help me to develop my inner man to hear Your
directions clearly and let the adventure begin.*

The Hard Way

TRACIE

> But if we confess our sins to him, he is faithful and just
> to forgive us and to cleanse us from every wrong.
>
> 1 JOHN 1:9 NLT

I dropped out of school at the age of fifteen. I was so busy trying to grow up that I never thought about the fact that I wouldn't know what to do when I finally got there. I had my son one month after my eighteenth birthday, not yet married and without any education. I looked into his eyes. He was six pounds and helpless without me. I began to wonder what his life would be like. Would he struggle the way that I had? What did I have to offer him?

I knew it would be hard to go back to school with a child, but what would happen to him if I didn't? When I looked into his eyes, I wanted to see a shining future full of every opportunity I could give him. I knew to get there I would have to work hard and set my sights high. He was my treasure. He was my reminder that each generation has a choice to define their destiny.

I went back to high school and graduated. Then I went on to college. I'm married now and have four great kids. I learned a lot the hard way and I don't recommend it, but I know that no matter what is in our past, we have a choice every day to either become what God has planned for us, or just to let another day slip by. When God looks at us, He feels the same way I do when I look into my son's eyes. He knows the great things we can achieve if given the opportunity; He does everything He can to make our choice easy, and then He leaves the choice up to us.

LIVE ON PURPOSE

Maybe you have made some mistakes. God wants to forgive you. First John 1:9 says that if you confess your sins, He is willing and just to forgive your sins and cleanse you from all unrighteousness. That verse was not written to sinners; it was written to Christians. Just because you're saved does not mean you are perfect. God's mercy is here for you. God's destiny is waiting for you.

PRAYER

Father God, I'm sorry. Forgive me.
Thank You for making me clean.
Help me to start fresh.
Help me to fulfill my destiny in You, in Jesus' name.

Knowing the Word

MIKE

{ *If ye abide in me, and my words abide in you, ye shall
ask what ye will, and it shall be done unto you.* }

JOHN 15:7 KJV

The Lord often confirms His Word to me in natural
circumstances. It encourages me that He is so
aware of every detail of my life and that He is
seeking to teach me more about Him. Recently I have been
studying and memorizing Scriptures. By knowing the Word,
it has made me much more aware of God's presence in my
life. The other morning I was studying Romans 4:17. It
talks about how God calls things that do not exist as if they
already existed. It's an example to us of how faith works.
While at work that day, I asked one of my associates in
accounting a question. As she was turning to answer, I
glanced at the digital screen she was working on. The
screen showed 417—the same number of the verse I was
studying! I felt like the Holy Spirit quickened that verse to

me again at that moment. Later on that day I was watching a minister on television. During his message he said that his favorite verse was Romans 4:17. It was like God again confirmed to me how important this verse is in my life.

On another occasion I was talking to a friend who was struggling with a drinking problem but wanted to get his life right with God. He was under a lot of condemnation about wasting so much time in his life. The Scripture that came to mind was Romans 8:28 which talks about how God will work all things together for good to those that are called according to His purpose. I told my friend that God could use what had happened in his life for good. When we pulled into the parking lot, there was a car parked next to us with a license plate that read 19K 828.

LIVE ON PURPOSE

Mike has disciplined himself to read and study the Word. Because his thoughts are on the Word, God can speak to him and teach him on a regular basis, even through natural circumstances. When Mike needed a Scripture to minister to a friend, that Word came back up in him at just the right time. If you feel like your communication with God could be better, start by reading the Word of God consistently.

PRAYER

Lord, in Jesus' name, help me to be diligent to read Your Word. I know there are many things in this world that are trying to get my attention. Help me to filter them out and make quality time for Your Word every day. I want to know more about You and Your ways.

Sensitive to the Spirit

REBECKA

> *What I'm getting at, friends, is that you should simply*
> *keep on doing what you've done from the beginning.*
> *When I was living among you, you lived in responsive*
> *obedience. Now that I'm separated from you, keep it up.*
> *Better yet, redouble your efforts. Be energetic in your*
> *life of salvation, reverent and sensitive before God.*
>
> PHILIPPIANS 2:12 MESSAGE

During my last year of high school in Sweden, I was leaving one afternoon and just wanted to go home and relax. I felt the Holy Spirit speak to me. He told me to ask my teacher if our Christian school group could come to my class to talk about Christianity. Since I wanted to go home, I thought I could do that tomorrow, but then I felt it was important to do it right away, so I did. I had to wait for my teacher quite a long time and I almost got irritated. I asked the Holy Spirit if it was really necessary to do it today, and I felt like He said it was.

The next day my teacher told me what happened. After I had left his office he received a phone call from a man with a request to come to the class and tell about a specific church, whereby he had answered that he already had students coming to talk about Christianity. Hearing that made me so thankful to the Holy Spirit, because He knew everything about this, and that was the reason why it was so important to see my teacher that specific afternoon. By being sensitive and obeying the Holy Spirit, I had the opportunity to present Jesus Christ to my class, and I know that they know how to get saved.

LIVE ON PURPOSE

The Holy Spirit will never force you to do anything, but if you are open, He will lead you in adventures that in your natural mind you will not even imagine. First Corinthians 2:19 tells us that no eye has seen, no ear has heard, no mind has conceived what God has prepared for those who love him, but God has revealed it to us by His Spirit. The Spirit of God, or the Holy Spirit, wants to reveal these blessings and adventures to you. That's why Paul admonished the Christians in Philippi to be "sensitive before God."

PRAYER

Lord, please help me to be sensitive to Your Spirit. I know that by spending time with You through Your Word, talking to You, and listening to You, I will grow closer to You. Even if I miss Your leading, I ask You to teach me how to discern Your voice from my own thoughts, in Jesus' name.

No Fear, Part 1

SARAH

> *Let no one despise your youth, but be an*
> *example to the believers in word, in conduct,*
> *in love, in spirit, in faith, in purity.*
>
> 1 TIMOTHY 4:12 NKJV

During one summer I went on a mission trip to Ghana, Africa. It was a life-changing trip, but it was not easy. In the middle of the trip the leaders decided they were going to take us up into the Northern Mountain villages to minister. As we were driving to the villages, they told us we were going to be dropped off two by two at different villages to spend the night and minister the following day. Inside I was freaking out! Then they told me that I was being dropped off with the youngest girl on our trip who had never been on missions before! As I began to pray in tongues, I thought, *What am I doing here?*

As the bus drove away, I tried to be brave even though my heart was pounding in my ears. I met the pastors of the church and immediately they asked me to preach in their church service the next morning. I had never preached a full sermon before! Then they told me the service lasted four hours!

That night during dinner, which was some sort of grass soup I swallowed down, I wondered what I would speak on the next day. It got dark quickly, and I crawled into my mosquito net, lay on the mat on the ground, and tried to sleep. I tossed and turned as I tried to think about what to speak on the next day.

Then God spoke a verse to my heart from Jeremiah 1:6. In that verse Jeremiah said to God, "But Lord, I cannot speak, I am a youth!" But God said, "'Do not say I am only a youth, for you will go to the people I send you and whatever I tell you, you will speak, do not be afraid of their faces for I am with you to deliver you,' says the Lord." God began to show me in His Word what I was to speak on the next day.

LIVE ON PURPOSE

Sarah had already learned to trust God, and even though she felt unqualified, she still had faith in God. When God spoke to her heart, she knew she would be able to minister to these people. Even though Sarah was young and had never preached an entire sermon, her relationship with God was close and she knew where to draw her strength. Don't let anything hold you back from your call. It's not your age that's important; it's your relationship with God.

PRAYER

Father, even though I may be young and unqualified, I trust You to give me Your favor and ability for what You've called me to do. In ministry, in school, in my career, thank You for giving me Your provision, in Jesus' name.

No Fear, Part 2

SARAH

> For God did not give us a spirit of timidity (of cowardice,
> of craven and cringing and fawning fear), but [He has
> given us a spirit] of power and of love and of calm and
> well-balanced mind and discipline and self-control.
>
> 2 TIMOTHY 1:7 AMP

Just as I started to drift off to sleep, I began to hear the sound of bongo drums beating. They got louder and then I heard people chanting. We had been told that some of the people in Africa called upon evil spirits. Fear began to try to grip me. Then God's Word came to my heart from 2 Timothy 1:7 which says that God has not given me a spirit of fear but of power, love, and a sound mind. That night all that had been implanted in my heart over the years I have been a Christian came out. I bound that spirit of fear, pleaded the blood of Jesus, and declared His angels' protection over me.

The devil will do whatever he can to get you to cower in fear so you won't do what God wants you to do. But don't let the enemy intimidate you! Jesus Christ lives in you! Greater is He that is in *you* than he that is in the world (1 John 4:4).

When I woke up the next morning I felt butterflies in my stomach, but I continued to speak the Word over myself. When it was my time to speak, the Lord gave me the words to say. People got healed and saved! After the service the minister told me that the message I spoke to them was exactly what their congregation needed.

Fear comes in all shapes and sizes. Yet you cannot allow the spirit of fear to keep you from fulfilling your destiny. Step out today! Do something you have never done before and you will see things you have never seen before. Remember, God is with you!

LIVE ON PURPOSE

Adventure truly begins in God. There is nothing like living in the Spirit, where you are trusting God every day and standing in awe of His power to deliver you. But the enemy will fight to keep you quiet and his weapon is fear. He knows that your faith in God will destroy him. Don't be fooled. With God nothing is impossible!

PRAYER

Father God, in Jesus' name, I bind the spirit of fear from my life. You gave me a spirit of love, power, and a sound mind. I make my decisions and my judgments based on Your leading inside of me and Your Word, not by the fear of man or any other thing.

Standing Strong

TRECIE

> *Death and life are in the power of the tongue,*
> *and those who love it will eat its fruit.*
>
> PROVERBS 18:21 NLV

In high school I worked on a televised A.M. program with several other students. On one occasion, my cohost remarked about a comment in the school newspaper: "The newspaper said that we look tired on the air and wear bags under our eyes like an accessory. They don't realize that we have to get up at 6 A.M. in the morning to get here on time!"

The national/international newsman agreed. "Yeah, I don't think the newspaper has a right to say anything until they mop up the misspellings in their articles."

My cohost turned back to me. "What do you have to say about it, Trecie?"

Underneath the glare of hot white lights, I had a decision to make. Either I could engage in rebutting the newspaper's remarks (besides, they had made some pretty nasty comments about us), or I could keep my peace and hold my tongue. Just when I was about to rip the newspaper department to shreds, the Holy Spirit arrested me with Ephesians 4:29:

> Let no corrupt communication proceed out of your mouth; but that which is good to the use of edifying, that it may minister grace unto the hearers.

Even though the hosts had not cursed, the communication was not edifying to the newspaper department. In this case, there were over 3000 "hearers"—students and faculty—waiting with bated breath for my response.

"No comment," I replied simply.

Just two words, but they spoke volumes. At the end of the broadcast, I said, "The A.M. cast and crew will take all comments from the newspaper into consideration."

My decision may not have won ratings, but it won God's approval. And in the end, His opinion is the only one that matters.

LIVE ON PURPOSE

It would have been easy for Trecie to go along with the crowd, but the Holy Spirit had a higher way. Trecie chose wisely and her life was blessed because of it. There's nothing like that feeling inside when you know you did the right thing. As you allow the Holy Spirit to lead you in everyday decisions, He can begin to bring greater opportunities across your path.

PRAYER

Father God, I ask You to help me today to make right decisions. When I am tempted to go along with other people who are not following Your ways, I'm asking that You give me Your resolve to stand strong for what's right, in Jesus' name.

Trust

TIM

> You, Lord, are the light that keeps me safe. I am not
> afraid of anyone. You protect me, and I have no fears.
> Brutal people may attack and try to kill me, but
> they will stumble. Fierce enemies may attack, but they
> will fall. Armies may surround me, but I won't be
> afraid; war may break out, but I will trust you.
>
> PSALM 27:1-3 CEV

When I was very young, I suffered from an older man molesting me. As you can imagine, this caused me to be full of pain and bitterness. I was in a shell and I didn't find any happiness in life or in myself either. I even contemplated suicide on several accounts and would have succeeded if Jesus hadn't intervened. I had accepted Jesus as my Savior, but I still was a long way off from forgiving and allowing my Lord to heal me completely. Then I remember going to the altar at church, weeping and crying out and telling the Lord that I was so tired of hurting; I just had to give it all up to Him. I told God that I was ready to let go of my will and allow Him to take away my pain and bitterness. At that moment I felt His presence wrap around me, and I felt a great weight lift off of me! It was like I was completely healed from all of the pain and darkness. Ever since then, God has continuously been restoring my joy and peace, and I know that I am a child of His. I know that He holds me in the palm of His hand and that with Him, all things truly are possible! I am free!

LIVE ON PURPOSE

Tim experienced a horrible trauma in his life. Even though he had accepted Jesus, he was still tormented by his past. God has given each of us a free will, and He has limited Himself to what we will allow Him to do in our lives. When Tim submitted everything to God, God was able to completely heal him. Are there areas where you need to receive more from God? Give Him an open door to bring what you need.

PRAYER

Father, I trust You and want to receive whatever
You have for me. Where I have been hurt in the past,
I ask You to heal those things in me. Help me to let go
of all unforgiveness and bitterness. Strengthen me
with power in my inner being. (Eph. 3:16.)
Give me Your peace and joy, in Jesus' name.

Cares and Burdens

DIANA

> Then Jesus said, "Come to me, all of you who are weary
> and carry heavy burdens, and I will give you rest."
>
> MATTHEW 11:28 NLT

I remember when it happened. It was during a meeting that opened with prayer. I had been struggling. I was going through one of those times in life when you're afraid to look at anyone because you know the tears will start to flow and you will not be able to shut them off. So many things were happening in my life that I had no control over. The problem? I was trying to control them and the outcome. But something happened during that time of prayer just before the meeting started. The vice president of our company was a man of God, and Jesus' presence would fill the room when he prayed. He would never waste words—it was never a casual prayer or something to do just because it's the thing to do. His purpose was to touch the throne room of God.

Listening with my eyes closed, I could see Jesus sitting in a beautiful place with green grass and trees all around. The peace of God came over me, and then Jesus opened up His arms welcoming me to come. I ran to Him and climbed in His lap. He put His arms around me and held me close. It was a feeling like no other. All my fears, concerns, and worries were absorbed by His loving embrace. It seemed like I was with Him for the longest time. I wanted that prayer to last, but it came to an end.

With my "Amen," I left everything in the capable hands of Jesus. Jesus let me see a glimpse of Him and held me, so that I would be assured that His arms are still reaching out. He wanted to carry my burdens, bear my pain, and take the cares of this world from me.

I go back at times when I need a reminder of His love. I just close my eyes and remember the day that I sat in my Father's lap. I can feel His arms around me. Someday I will get to sit in His lap and be in His presence for an eternity.

LIVE ON PURPOSE

God never wants us to worry or carry heavy burdens, but sometimes we do it without even thinking about it. Many times, just like Diana, we try to control things that we have no control over. When you recognize that you are under a heavy burden or care, take it before the Lord immediately. Philippians 4:6 says to be careful for nothing, but in everything by prayer and supplication with thanksgiving let your requests be made known unto God. Let Him take your cares today.

PRAYER

Father God, in Jesus' name, I choose to leave my cares with You. Thank You for Your care for me and for a place of rest for my soul. Help me to realize when I am taking on something I shouldn't so that I can stay in faith and at peace.

Controlling Emotions

KATE

> *If your sinful nature controls your mind,*
> *there is death. But if the Holy Spirit controls*
> *your mind, there is life and peace.*
>
> ROMANS 8:6 NLV

I love theatre. No, let me rephrase. I love good, "inspire me to work harder in my studies" theatre. I left my home in the Midwest to attend a small, private, liberal arts school in California. I had heard that they have a great dance program and a theatre department on the cutting edge of the theatre scene. When I arrived I found that the school was even better than I had hoped! And I was getting great roles.

I was so busy, however, that I wasn't investing in the people around me. It wasn't too long before I felt lonely, truly lonely, and I wanted to move home. I started looking into transferring to a school closer to home. I applied to the University of Minnesota, and when I was accepted I started to make all the necessary arrangements to transfer. One night when I was working on some paperwork, one of my only friends at the time asked to look at my transcripts. She discovered that I had taken enough units to enable me to graduate in three years. If I transferred, I would lose some credits and end up going to school longer. I had a decision in front of me and no idea which way to go. My family and I prayed for God's direction. I felt God speak inside my spirit. He told me to stay put. And you know, I hadn't learned all that I needed from that school. It's now a year later, and I am so thrilled that I didn't leave. I still miss my family, but God has opened one huge door for me, the possibility of staying in theatre beyond my college career.

LIVE ON PURPOSE

Kate's emotions started to affect her feelings about a place she originally felt peace about. It's easy to get caught up in how you feel, but God does not want you to live by your natural senses. He wants you to be led by the Spirit of God. When you are led by the Spirit, there is life and peace. The best way to recognize His voice is to spend time reading your Bible and in prayer. The Holy Spirit's leading will always line up with what the Word of God says. Get in the Word today and every day. The difference will amaze you.

PRAYER

Father, thank You for giving me Your Word. I know that I can trust it no matter what my feelings are. Speak to my heart through Your Word. I'm ready to listen, in Jesus' name.

God Knows

TRACIE

> *Remember the former things, those of long ago;*
> *I am God, and there is no other; I am God, and there is*
> *none like me. I make known the end from the beginning,*
> *from ancient times, what is still to come. I say: My*
> *purpose will stand, and I will do all that I please.*
>
> ISAIAH 46:9,10 NIV

Two years after I decided to not go to Bible school because of finances, God reminded me that I had made a commitment to Him. I had told Him I would go back to school when my family was out of debt. Really I had made that promise never expecting to get out of debt, yet there I was, $15,000 dollars paid off. I never understood why I needed to go back to school; I had been out of school for almost ten years. But I knew I wanted to please God. He said, *Go,* so I went.

The morning of graduation God showed me why it was so important that I had listened to His voice.

Alyssa, my six-year-old daughter, woke up with severe cramps. We rushed her to the emergency room on the morning of graduation. I never dreamed that five days later we would still be there. The tests showed an extra tube on her kidney which was causing a severe infection. The doctors advised surgery immediately and antibiotics for the rest of her life. But God had already prepared me. I had learned enough about God to know that He takes care of His kids. I had learned enough about the Bible in school and seen enough in my own life to know about God's faithfulness. God is always there! He is always waiting for us to come to Him so He can help. I prayed and I knew He would show Himself faithful as He always had. Alyssa never had to have surgery; they ran the tests again and were unable to find any reason why Alyssa got so sick. I learned a valuable lesson through all of that. Before God had ever spoken to me, He saw what we would go through. He knew how we needed to be prepared. And He sent the provision in advance.

LIVE ON PURPOSE

God knows the end from the beginning.
He knows what is coming, and He wants
you to overcome every challenge. You may
not understand exactly why God leads
you to do certain things, but when you
know it's God, follow His direction. He
always has your best in mind.

PRAYER

*Father God, forgive me if I have not followed
Your leading like I should. Help me to get back on
track with Your will for my life. Thank You for
Your provision in every area, in Jesus' name.*

Wisdom and Peace

GARY

> But the wisdom that is from above is first pure, then peaceable, gentle, willing to yield, full of mercy and good fruits, without partiality and without hypocrisy.
>
> JAMES 3:17 NKJV

After I graduated from college, I began praying about getting a good job. I visited the Employment Security Commission several times to check out their job listings. Every time I visited, it just seemed right on the inside that I should pursue a position with that agency, but there were no positions available. Since they were a government agency, most of their positions were temporary and somewhat "political." You had to know the right people, and I didn't know anyone there. The turnover rate with that agency was practically nonexistent. But I felt peace about applying there. Within six months, they created a new position and hired me. They eventually gave me an office in two different counties to run several government programs. The position included recruiting qualified applicants and sending them to school and negotiating job contracts with various employers. As a result, my job fulfilled the desire in my heart to work both in an office environment and in the field.

LIVE ON PURPOSE

Oftentimes God will lead you by the peace in your heart. James 3:17 tells us that the wisdom from above is first pure, then peaceable, gentle, full of mercy, impartial, and sincere. You may not understand exactly why you have peace about certain things, but when you have that peace inside, follow it. You will find that God's peace leads you to the desires of your heart.

PRAYER

Lord, thank You for leading me by the peace in my heart. Your wisdom is not harsh and demanding, but gentle and full of mercy. Help me to recognize Your peace and keep me from being deceived by my own thoughts or the enemy, in Jesus' name.

Visions From God

ANANIAS

Now there was a believer in Damascus named Ananias. The Lord spoke to him in a vision, calling, "Ananias!"

"Yes, Lord!" he replied.

The Lord said, "Go over to Straight Street, to the house of Judas. When you arrive, ask for Saul of Tarsus. He is praying to me right now. I have shown him a vision of a man named Ananias coming in and laying his hands on him so that he can see again."

"But Lord," exclaimed Ananias, "I've heard about the terrible things this man has done to the believers in Jerusalem! And we hear that he is authorized by the leading priests to arrest every believer in Damascus."

But the Lord said, "Go and do what I say. For Saul is my chosen instrument to take my message to the Gentiles and to kings, as well as to the people of Israel. And I will show him how much he must suffer for me."

So Ananias went and found Saul. He laid his hands on him and said, "Brother Saul, the Lord Jesus, who appeared to you on the road, has sent me so that you may get your sight back and be filled with the Holy Spirit." Instantly something like scales fell from Saul's eyes, and he regained his sight. Then he got up and was baptized.

ACTS 9:10-18 NLV

LIVE ON PURPOSE

In the Scriptures there are several instances when the Lord used visions to give direction. There was no question in Ananias's mind who was speaking to him. He knew it was God and His directions were very clear. Ananias was able to discuss this situation with the Lord. The Lord made sure Ananias understood why. God still uses visions today. It's not as often as leading by peace, but be open to the many ways God leads.

PRAYER

Father God, I am open to whatever way You choose to lead. Help me to understand clearly what You want me to do, in Jesus' name.

Speak Life

SUSAN

{
*But I say to you that for every idle word men
may speak, they will give account of it in the day of
judgment. For by your words you will be justified,
and by your words you will be condemned."*

MATTHEW 12:36,37 NKJV
}

I went to church one Sunday night and heard a
preacher talk about the importance of your words.
That night I went over my notes because his message
made me evaluate my own life. In the middle of the night I
had a vision that I was being led by an angel through the
mist. I came to a staircase and went up to a loft type of
room. I noticed a man at my side. He was dressed in very
plain clothes. As I looked at him, I saw that his eyes were
soft and deep. His face seemed to be very old yet beautiful
at the same time. His presence brought great comfort to
me. I believe He was the Holy Spirit. The room was full of
people dressed in robes. Their faces appeared to be perfect

and they were talking and laughing. There was an amazing sense of peace and joy that I cannot explain. One of the people turned to me and said, "How are things on the earth?" In my mind I formed my response and it was something like this: "Are you kidding? Compared to this, things are lousy on the earth!" Before I got the words out, the others seemed to know what I was going to say. They motioned to me not to say it, but it was too late. I could not stop the words from coming out. Immediately I was falling but I felt the Lord holding me in His hand as I fell. I awoke in my bed. My body felt heavy as if I was gone and I had returned to wake it up. The presence of God was very strong in the room and I lay very still. The Lord spoke to me and said two words, *Speak life*. The words resounded through my whole being. For the next three days, I could feel the presence of the Lord was very strong on me. It was an experience and lesson that changed my life and my words forever.

LIVE ON PURPOSE

The power of your words can put you over or take you under. Proverbs 18:21 says that life and death are in the power of the tongue. James 3 says that the tongue is set on fire by hell and that it sets the course of your life. You need the Holy Spirit to help you "speak life." Ask Him to show you when you are saying negative things, and let the Word of God be your guide on how to talk about yourself and others.

PRAYER

Lord, I really need Your help when it comes to my words. I know my words will set the course of my life. Please let me know when I have crossed the line in my speech. Help me to speak good things, and if I can't, then help me to keep my mouth shut, in Jesus' name.

Guilt

A L I

Therefore, [there is] now no condemnation (no adjudging guilty of wrong) for those who are in Christ Jesus, who live [and] walk not after the dictates of the flesh, but after the dictates of the Spirit. For the law of the Spirit of life [which is] in Christ Jesus [the law of our new being] has freed me from the law of sin and of death.

ROMANS 8:1,2 AMP

During spring break of my freshman year I went to Bolivia on a missions trip with my school. While I was there, I was seeking to know God better but not to the full extent of what I probably should have. One morning after our group finished performing a drama to an outside crowd, I felt like God was telling me to talk to some girls who were watching us. Now, I had never really led someone to Christ, but while I was there I had to step out of my comfort zone. While I was talking to these girls, they opened up and wanted to know Jesus Christ. They had no idea who He was, but by just watching our drama and realizing the love we had for Him, they wanted to know Him too. It amazed me. There and then they accepted Christ. I didn't have to be a perfect person to be a witness. I only had to be willing to step out in faith. Even though I didn't feel like I was the greatest Christian, God chose to use me. God can work through you no matter where you are with Him. That experience totally changed my relationship with God. Every day now I seek Him and He leads me to love and life. He can do anything through you if you are open.

LIVE ON PURPOSE

We may have our own ideas about what kind of Christian we are supposed to be, and the enemy is always trying to put shame on us, but Romans 8 tells us that there is no condemnation in Christ. We are free, but that doesn't mean we always feel free. Being free is part of walking by faith. When we feel guilt for not being good enough, recognize that thought is not from God. He never gives up on us and often works through us when we least expect it!

PRAYER

Father, in Jesus' name, I refuse to accept guilt and condemnation for not being good enough. I am the righteousness of God in Christ Jesus. It's in Jesus that I have been made free—free from sin, condemnation, shame, and fear. Every day I am growing stronger in Christ. His favor and grace give me the abilities and strength I need to be successful in every area.

The Wait

JONATHAN

{ *But they that wait upon the Lord*
shall renew their strength. }

ISAIAH 40:31 KJV

A few years ago I struggled severely with chronic pain in my left hip. I went to several doctors and none of them could figure out what was wrong. Finally, they labeled it as tendonitis, prescribing heavy doses of an anti-inflammatory. I continually prayed for God's healing, not seeing any results for some time. Discouragement tried to grip my heart, but I steadily put my hope in Jesus for my healing. I recall the day when I had only five pills left for the pain and I proclaimed, "Lord, this is the last bottle of anti-inflammatory for this pain. I *am* healed!" Each day I would proclaim my healing with each pill. The last pill had been taken, and that day I received healing in my body. That day in chapel, the speaker asked if we needed healing in our bodies. I knew it was a divine appointment as I jumped to my feet. I have not taken another pill since that day. God miraculously healed me.

LIVE ON PURPOSE

First Corinthians 13 says that we see through a glass darkly and that we only know in part. In this age, you will not know everything, but the God you serve does. If you stick close to Him through fellowship and the Scriptures, He will take care of you through discouraging times. Jonathan "steadily" put his hope in Jesus and he received what he believed. Are you waiting on God for something? Don't give up. Stay steady and keep your faith in Jesus.

PRAYER

Lord, I will not give up on Your promises to me. My trust and my faith are in You, no matter what it looks like in the natural. I will wait on You and You will renew my strength, in Jesus' name.

Faith for Small Things

ALICE

> *But without faith it is impossible to please him: for he*
> *that cometh to God must believe that he is, and that*
> *he is a rewarder of them that diligently seek him.*
>
> HEBREWS 11:6 KJV

L ast summer while visiting my family, my aunt
pulled out lots of old pictures for us to look at, and
to my delight, I saw that she had some school
pictures of both my siblings and me. This was quite
surprising for me because my family had a house fire that
destroyed our childhood pictures.

Later that afternoon my sister went to a store to
make copies of our pictures. She wasn't able to make the
copies and when she returned home, my little picture was
missing. Well, right then I put my foot down and said, "No,
it is not lost." I prayed that God would show me where it
was. I called the store and asked if they had found the tiny
picture. The answer was "no." Later that evening I went to

the store to look for myself. I had the cleaning crew called and still the answer was "no." I began to walk the aisles of the store and pray. After about 40 minutes with no success, I started heading toward the door. All of the sudden I heard over the intercom, "Would the lady who's looking for a school picture please come to the photography area?" I ran over, and there stood a man over six feet tall with the picture in hand!

This man felt that God told him to go through nearly three feet of trash, piece by piece. At the very bottom of the trash he found it, and it was in spotless condition. He told me that he was a Christian and he felt in his heart that he needed to look as thoroughly as he could. I told him that I was a Christian and that God had used his obedience to answer my prayer. He was so blessed that God had used him, and so was I!

LIVE ON PURPOSE

A picture may seem like a small thing to you, but to God it was very important. He honored Alice's faith by sending someone to find her picture at the bottom of the trash. And God will honor your faith even in small things. Your well-being is very important to Him. Take time to put your faith in God for big and small things.

PRAYER

Father, I will believe You to help me in small things and big things. You are pleased when I release my faith and trust You to bring those things into my life. I purpose in my heart to bring these issues to You instead of trying to do them in my own strength, in Jesus' name.

A Word From God

NATALIE

> *But the manifestation of the Spirit is given to every*
> *man to profit withal. For to one is given by the*
> *Spirit the word of wisdom; to another the*
> *word of knowledge by the same Spirit…*
>
> 1 CORINTHIANS 12:7,8 KJV

One Sunday night in a church group, God spoke to me through the group leader. I had been struggling through some things with one of my friends. I had been growing stronger in the Lord and my friend had not. We just weren't connecting and things were going wrong. The Word given to me said to guard my heart. The group leader couldn't stress enough for me to guard my heart. A week or so later, I found out some negative things about this friend. She started treating me really awful. She said some extremely mean things that could have hurt me. But I remembered what God had said to me that Sunday night. I was able to move on and not be hurt. By guarding my heart, God helped me through it.

LIVE ON PURPOSE

God has given spiritual gifts to help you. In Natalie's situation, God gave her a word of wisdom. Oftentimes you are so close to the situation that it is difficult for God to get His point across to you. He may send trusted mentors and leaders into your life with a word from heaven just for you. This does not mean that other people should control you, but when you receive a word from God through another person, you should judge it and pray about it yourself. Natalie was prepared when her friend turned against her. God knew it was going to happen and sent a word to Natalie in a way she could receive it. These spiritual gifts are found in 1 Corinthians 12-14 and include other manifestations such as healing and miracles. It would be good for you to know about each one of God's gifts so that if you need help, you will understand what God is doing and be ready to receive it or give it to someone else.

PRAYER

Father, I want to know as much about You as possible.
As a supernatural God, You do supernatural things.
Help me to understand Your ways so that I don't
miss out when You are trying to help me and so that
I can help others when You need me to, in Jesus' name.

Changes

ERIK

I grew up with three guys. We were great friends for a lot of years, but due to some differences we stopped hanging out. I guess that was okay since they were doing things I really didn't want to do, but I missed having close friends. About this same time, my family changed churches. I had to meet new people, which was hard at first, but I met a guy who has become one of my best friends. He is a godly guy and we both have a lot of the same interests. Just when I was having fun and getting to know everyone, we switched churches again. It was like starting all over. The great thing is, my friend and I are still good friends. Now at this new church I have a great pastor and have made more friends. Even though I have gone through a lot of changes the last couple of years, God has shown me some things about Him. He was watching out for me every time things changed. I lost friends that weren't so good for me and I met friends that know God. I kept good friends, even though I moved farther away from them. God does work things out.

LIVE ON PURPOSE

Change can make us uncomfortable, especially when we have to start over with relationships. True friendships take time to develop and no one likes to feel alone. When you are dealing with change, remember Psalm 37:23. When you belong to God, He orders your steps. He is watching out for you. He'll even tell you what groups to hook up with if you will ask Him. If you have been feeling alone, make sure you take those feelings to God in prayer and ask Him to help you find the right friends.

PRAYER

Father God, in Jesus' name, I want my confidence to be so strong in You that when change comes, it will not shake me. Strengthen me in my inner man. Thank You for ordering my steps and bringing divine connections across my path. I'm open to Your direction in my life, and if that means change, thank You for preparing me for it.

Ministry

HANNA

> All this comes from God. He is the One Who brought us to Himself when we hated Him. He did this through Christ. Then He gave us the work of bringing others to Him.
>
> 2 CORINTHIANS 5:18 NLV

One day, several years ago, I was hanging out with four of my friends. We were just talking about God and heaven and how God will save anyone. Well, one of my friends was not saved and she asked me if she could be saved. I told her that of course she could. I said, "Do you want to be saved?" She said "yes." A little bit later my sister, my other friends, and I prayed with her. After we prayed she said, "I'm so glad I did that!" Even though I'm not a minister, I know I made a difference.

LIVE ON PURPOSE

You, like Hanna, may not have the title of "minister," but we've all been given the ministry of reconciliation. God wants all of us to bring others to Him, because He loves everyone. All you need to do is follow the Holy Spirit's lead. Just to be prepared, a great Scripture to memorize is Romans 10:9-10. It gives two simple steps for someone to be saved:

Confess with your mouth that Jesus is Lord. Believe in your heart that God raised Him from the dead.

If you have an opportunity to lead someone to Jesus, just have them do those two things. And even if they are not ready to pray, just the fact that you talked to them about the Lord plants a seed in their life. Telling others about God is the greatest adventure.

PRAYER

Father God, help me to be aware of anyone who needs to know about You. I'm willing to talk to others. When You open the door, give me courage and wisdom to know what I should do, in Jesus' name.

Healing Direction

ANGEL

> *Whether you turn to the right or to the left,*
> *your ears will hear a voice behind you, saying,*
> *"This is the way; walk in it."*
>
> ISAIAH 30:21 NIV

I remember taking naps whenever I could get a chance during my first year at college. I had fatigue, allergies, nagging back pain, stomach problems, headaches, and much more wrong with my body. I gained 25 pounds within the first three months of college and had to go to the chiropractor once a week for therapy. I went to the doctor. I even went to a back specialist. I tried natural remedies, but nothing seemed to help. Desperate and frustrated I remember standing in a prayer line my freshman year and hearing God say, *You are healed.* Now, years later, I am completely healed, and as I look back over the years, I see how God had me "walk out" my healing. He led me to a women's conference in Palm Springs where I met a Christian trainer who taught me how to eat healthy and get in shape. He led me to a Christian doctor who helped me cleanse my system and got me feeling like a brand-new person. Over time, by applying these practical lifestyle changes, God's power brought about my healing. Sometimes miracles must be walked out. I am thankful that the Holy Spirit is with us to show us the way.

LIVE ON PURPOSE

The Scriptures say in Proverbs 20:27 that your
spirit is the candle of the Lord. Your spirit is
where God communicates with you. You have a
body, you have a soul (your mind, will, and
emotions), and you have a spirit. When you are
born again your spirit is recreated in Christ Jesus.
You are a new creature in Christ. The Spirit of
God, or the Holy Spirit, can communicate with
you constantly. He will only lead you, however,
as much as you allow Him to. He will never
violate your free will. Just as Angel was led by
God in several very practical ways to receive her
healing, the Holy Spirit will communicate with
you through your spirit the things you need to
succeed in your life. Spending time reading the
Word, in prayer, and listening gives you the
opportunity to hear God's direction.

PRAYER

*Father God, I want You to know that I am open
to Your leading. I welcome Your presence and Your
communication with me. Please help me to be conscious
of what You are saying to me, in Jesus' name.*

An Example

CALEB

> *Don't let anyone look down on you because you*
> *are young, but set an example for the believers*
> *in speech, in life, in love, in faith and in purity.*
>
> 1 TIMOTHY 4:12 NIV

At one Wednesday night service there was a girl who needed a job. She was having a job interview the next day and asked if someone would pray that she would get the job. I was pretty young compared to some of the other people there, but I felt God told me to pray for her. I followed what I felt God was telling me to do and prayed for her. My prayer may not have been as well spoken as someone else's, but I know enough about God to pray when someone needs help. The next service I found out she got the job. It wasn't because of my great prayer, but because of God.

LIVE ON PURPOSE

Your age in the natural does not really matter to God. You can be young and have great wisdom in God, and you can be old and have very little wisdom in God. It depends on how much time you have taken to know God. David was very young when he defeated Goliath. Some historians say that he was only 16, yet he had more courage and faith in God to go up against a 13-foot giant than the men who had been fighting for years. Why? David had spent his youth alone with God while he watched his father's sheep. God helped him kill a lion and a bear. He knew God would help him defeat the giant as well. He knew God. He didn't have confidence in his own strength. His confidence was in God working through him. You can be an example to others no matter how old you are, just by getting to know God.

PRAYER

Lord, I know that my success depends on how well I follow You. I accept the challenge of setting an example to other believers. I ask You to help me to be bold in You and have confidence in You working through me, in Jesus' name.

Draw Near

> *Come near to God, and God will come near*
> *to you. You sinners, clean sin out of your lives.*
> *You who are trying to follow God and the world*
> *at the same time, make your thinking pure.*
>
> JAMES 4:8 NCV

I remember when I wasn't that close to God. I wasn't as happy as I am now. I just wanted to hang out with my older friends at church instead of going to the class that was specifically for my age. I thought I wanted to be more like these friends, but even though I was hanging around with them, I still wasn't happy. I always had a feeling that I needed to go to that class. I guess that was the Holy Spirit drawing me in. One day I did go. When I went there the first time, the pastor quoted a Scripture I have never forgotten. It answered why God wasn't close to me before. The Scripture is James 4:8. It says that when you draw close to God, He will draw close to you. God was waiting on me. All that time I was thinking the wrong thing. Now if I start feeling a long way from God, I just draw near. I talk to God and read my Bible. Then God draws near to me. It's great.

LIVE ON PURPOSE

Amanda thought that God did not want to be close to her. She was searching for a place to belong in friends instead of in God. But people will never satisfy your soul; only God can. When she realized that God was waiting on her, everything changed. God is waiting on you as well. He will never violate your free will. If you want to be closer to God, just draw near. Draw near today.

PRAYER

Lord, I want to be closer to You. Help me not to be distracted by the things of this world so that it steals my time with You. Help me to keep the right priorities in my life, in Jesus' name.

Never Forsaken

AARON

Once I was young, and now I am old.
Yet I have never seen the godly forsaken,
nor seen their children begging for bread.

PSALM 37:25 NLT

One semester I was doing an internship in New York City. I didn't know if New York was where I was going to stay, but I was trusting God to lead me. I was living on my own and I was low on cash a lot. One evening I was walking around the city hanging out. I was really hungry and only had a little cash in my pocket. It wasn't enough to get much to eat, and it's all I had until my next paycheck. My family was miles away, and I didn't know anyone who could help me out. I was so hungry. As I was walking I saw some money on the ground! It was just enough to buy a combo meal at Wendy's. That food tasted so good. It was delicious. God provides. He is so wonderful!

LIVE ON PURPOSE

If you belong to God, then He has made a promise to you that He will never leave you and never forsake you. That means no matter what you are facing, you can go to God and remind Him of His promise. When you remind Him of His promise, He recognizes your faith, and that pleases God. Numbers 23:19 tells us that God is not man that He should lie, nor a son of man that He should change His mind. What He said in His Word, He will do. Aaron could have blamed God for not taking care of him, but instead he went for a walk and trusted God anyway. God came through. It wasn't an eight-course meal at the finest restaurant in town, but it was what he needed at the time. Sometimes God's answer is not exactly what you expected, but it's what you need when you need it. If you are lacking in some area, find your promise in the Scriptures and bring it before the Lord. He is your provider.

PRAYER

Father God, Your Word says that You will never leave me and never forsake me. In the areas where I feel I am lacking, I am coming to You as my Father and my provider to take care of me. Thank You for Your provision, in Jesus' name.

Attitude

LAUREN

For the word of God is living and powerful, and sharper than any two-edged sword, piercing even to the division of soul and spirit, and of joints and marrow, and is a discerner of the thoughts and intents of the heart.

HEBREWS 4:12 NKJV

I went on a mission trip to Bolivia. I was very excited to do something for God. We were about five days into the trip and this day was an all-day trip. I hadn't personally led anyone to Christ since we arrived, and it was starting to get to me. That day my best friend, Libby, helped someone get saved for the first time. I was so happy for her, but at the same time it kind of got me down. During my quiet time that day, I was praying to God and He gave me the verse of Philemon 1:7. It says, "We have great joy and consolation in your love because the hearts of the people have been refreshed by you." This helped me to realize that you don't have to personally lead someone to the Lord, that simply sharing His Word with them will refresh their hearts. And that changed my heart. It wasn't all about me; it was about sharing Jesus. The rest of the mission trip I had a much better attitude towards what I did.

LIVE ON PURPOSE

God is always ready to take you to a new level. Lauren was trained and ready to be a witness for the Lord, but her attitude was not in the right place. It was in her quiet time with God that He was able to reveal to her what was wrong. Hebrews 4:12 says that the Word of God is a discerner of the thoughts and intents of the heart. When you spend time with God and in His Word, He is able to take you to new levels in your spiritual walk. No one is perfect; everyone has to walk out their salvation, renew their minds, and keep their flesh under. Let God take you to a new level. Spend a little time with Him.

PRAYER

Father God, I do not want to be stagnant in my relationship with You. I want to continually be moving to a new level. If there are areas that I need to focus in on, I ask You to reveal them to me and to help me, in Jesus' name.

Willing and Obedient

RENOULTE

{
If you are willing and obedient,
you shall eat the good of the land.

ISAIAH 1:19 NKJV
}

I remember standing outside taking pictures with my family; I had finally made it. I was so happy. No more long nights cramming for tests and, best of all, no more mac & cheese as my main source of nutrition. Then it hit me. I was reminded that I was the first in the history of my family to graduate from college. The look in my grandmother's and father's eyes—they were so proud of the sacrifices that had been made for me to get this far. I remember thinking to myself, *Why me? Why did it take so long for someone to make it this far?* Then God reminded me that it was all the times I cried out to Him when I wanted to give up. All the times I trusted Him and pressed through when the money was low, when I had to hitch rides to class, when I had to walk a mile and a half to get to work in the snow (no joke). He said that because I decided not to quit and to trust Him, He would end the cycle of poverty in my family, and those after me would be blessed because of my obedience to serve Him.

Shortly after that I received a job with a Fortune 500 company and did very well. I was able to make more money by myself in one year than both of my parents ever made with both of them working. My wife and children have never seen the tough times that I went through as the oldest of six children—when there was not enough money for food, or when the utilities were cut off and we had to boil water in the morning to take a bath. I am so grateful to God that He guided me and gave me the strength to make it. I am glad that He is using me to do great things for my family and others who are in need. When I was young I used to think, *Where is God? Why don't we have more? Why are times so hard? Why does it seem that those who have no reverence for God continue to prosper?* But in the end, God has blessed me beyond my wildest dreams, and it is true that the willing and obedient will eat the good of the land.

LIVE ON PURPOSE

Everyone has opportunities to quit, but when
God is leading and directing you, why quit?
Because it's hard? God will make a way where
there is no way, even if it seems like things are
too hard. Get in His Word and find Scriptures
that you can stand on. Don't let the enemy
talk you into defeat. With God on your side,
you can overcome every obstacle.

PRAYER

*Father God, help me to stay strong through tough times.
I know with You on my side I can overcome even if things
get difficult. Even if it seems there is no way, I know
You will make a way. I am determined to be willing and
obedient to all You called me to do, in Jesus' name.*

God's Will or Your Will?

BILLY

> *Let no man deceive himself. If any man*
> *among you seemeth to be wise in this world,*
> *let him become a fool, that he may be wise.*
> *For the wisdom of this world is foolishness with God.*
>
> 1 CORINTHIANS 3:18,19 KJV

I remember just over two years ago I was set on attending college in Colorado, hundreds of miles away from home. There was a college just a couple of miles from my house which I had never considered attending. I felt like God was telling me to consider this college in my hometown. I had applied and was accepted to both colleges, but was still set on going to Colorado in the fall. I fought against the leading in my heart for many months, but when it came down to making a committed decision, I chose to attend the college in my hometown. I just knew inside that it was God's will. Now I am currently pursing a medical career through Christian missions as my future occupation. God has prepared an amazing yet challenging future of leading people to Christ, while focusing on people's physical needs through the medical aspect. After one year at this college, I have already led a mission team and have been selected as a regional coordinator to train leaders of mission teams throughout Asia. As I look back now, I wonder what I would have settled for had I chosen Colorado.

LIVE ON PURPOSE

Hearing God's voice is not as difficult as you think. Oftentimes, it's your own thoughts that drown Him out. Billy knew in his heart what God wanted him to do, but his own imaginations kept him struggling for months with this decision. Sometimes you have to get real with yourself and sift through what *you want to happen* and the leading in your heart. God is for you, not against you. Look at what He says in Jeremiah 29:11 NKJV: "For I know the thoughts that I think toward you, says the Lord, thoughts of peace and not of evil, to give you a future and a hope." His plan always has your happiness and success in mind.

PRAYER

Father God, forgive me for overriding Your leading with my own thoughts. I don't want to imagine Your will for my life. I want the real thing. Give me the discernment to tell the difference, in Jesus' name.

Direction From God

ROBIN

*Roll your works upon the Lord
[commit and trust them wholly to Him;
He will cause your thoughts to
become agreeable to His will, and]
so shall your plans be established and succeed.*

PROVERBS 16:3 AMP

When my husband and I first got married we were both working at the same place, but soon I knew it was time for me to move on. I applied at two different places and got interviews for both. The first job wanted to hire me right away. They were willing to pay me what I wanted and let me choose my position. Although the offer was too good to be true, I knew in my heart that God told me I would be working at the other place. So I held out. The second job had a strenuous interview process that took several weeks. In the meantime the first job kept calling me back and raising the offer! It sounded better and better and was harder to resist, but I knew where God wanted me. Finally, after almost a month, I got the call: I was offered the job and they agreed to pay me the final offer of the first job. It was a wonderful job with more benefits than I can mention.

By the time I left I was making much more than I could have at the first job. Plus God worked many things out for me in the course of that season there, not to mention all the wonderful people I met and experiences I had. I don't know what the other path would have been like, but I know I chose the best path for me.

LIVE ON PURPOSE

You may be tempted to let circumstances dictate the will of God for your life. Hold out. If Robin had taken what looked good on the outside, she would have missed God's best. When God wants to give you direction, He speaks to your spirit and it stays with you. You'll know what to do, because it will be strong in your spirit. That kind of leading from the Lord is easier to recognize when you have spent time in prayer and in the Word. In John 16:13 it says that the Holy Spirit will tell us things to come, but if you go back to John 15, the Word talks about how important it is to abide in Jesus and let His Word abide in you. So if you've struggled hearing His voice in your spirit, stock up on the Word—abide in Jesus. It really does make a difference.

PRAYER

Father God, I want to hear You in my spirit.
I commit myself to read and study Your Word.
Give me insight into Your Word and into my future.
Thank You that I have the Holy Spirit and that
He will show me things to come, in Jesus' name.

Giving by the Spirit

PATRICK

> *Give, and [gifts] will be given to you; good measure,*
> *pressed down, shaken together, and running over, will they*
> *pour into [the pouch formed by] the bosom [of your robe*
> *and used as a bag]. For with the measure you deal out*
> *[with the measure you use when you confer benefits*
> *on others], it will be measured back to you.*
>
> LUKE 6:38 AMP

God got a hold of me the end of my senior year, and that summer He told me to go to a Christian university. My dad was absolutely against it and refused to pay for anything if I went there. He didn't want me going to school to be a preacher since I was going to major in Theology. I had no idea how I would make it, but I knew that was where the Holy Spirit was leading me. I had already missed the deadlines for scholarships, so I filled out an application for a student loan and I was approved for half of the tuition. All I had saved from working that summer was $800. It did not look good. Suddenly the gift of faith rose up in me that no matter what, I would go to that university. God would make a way. So I packed my car and went. I enrolled and the admissions department told me I could go if I paid the remaining balance off in monthly payments for the rest of the school year. I took a school-paid job scrubbing dorm showers for $125 a month, but I needed a lot more to make my payments.

That first week of school I went to church and the minister spoke on sowing seed for your need. God prompted me to sow the entire $800 I had saved towards their building fund. Two days later my mom called me and said my dad had a sudden change of heart and agreed to pay towards my tuition. That money along with the $125 from my job left me with a little extra! My dad continued to pay part of my tuition every month for the next two years. The key to being led by God is obeying when you know it is Him. He provides after you obey, because that is faith.

LIVE ON PURPOSE

When you sow a seed, it releases a spiritual principle to work on your behalf. Luke 6:38 clearly outlines the principles of seedtime and harvest as well as many other Scriptures. It's God's way of releasing blessings into your life. Second Corinthians 9:7 in the Amplified version says to give as you have purposed in your heart, not reluctantly or under compulsion because God loves a joyful giver. Patrick did not give because he felt pressure to help the church, but because God prompted him. He had joy because he had faith in God's leading. When you give, ask God what you should do and remember Luke 6:38. Release your faith that when you sow, it will be given back to you much more.

PRAYER

Father, in Jesus' name, show me where I should give and what I should give. Thank You that when I give, it is given back to me pressed down, shaken together, and running over.

What God Wants

GARY

{ *Therefore I say unto you, What things soever*
ye desire, when ye pray, believe that ye
receive them, and ye shall have them. }

MATTHEW 11:24 KJV

After college graduation, I set aside three days to seek the Lord as to whether I should leave or stay in the area where I graduated. I had great peace every time I thought about staying, but I would become anxious whenever I thought about leaving. At that time I was very involved in a church full of college students and young families. Inside, I felt good about staying, and I also felt that I should start believing God for a house. I asked the Lord for three specific things about this house. First, I wanted an addition to the house that I could rent out. Second, I wanted the house to have a good view of the mountains. And third, I wanted the house to be close to town and yet have no city sounds and noises. One year later exactly to the month, my house with the three specific conditions came to pass and yet it was much more than what I had asked for. Amazingly, I didn't even have money for a down payment, but God worked it out.

LIVE ON PURPOSE

God will not only lead you directionally, but He will also lead you in what things to have faith for. It is God's desire that you prosper and be in health as listed in 3 John 2 and many other Scriptures. If you will set aside time to seek God on practical issues, He will direct you to believe for specific things. It may be a certain car, a scholarship, a job, or, as in Gary's case, a house. Take some time today and seek God about what things He desires for you to have. Then pray and believe God to bring them in your life.

PRAYER

Lord, I know You have good things in store for me. Please lead me as I believe You for the things that are in my heart. I want to have Your best in my life, in Jesus' name.

Understanding Love

SHEILA

> *Greater love hath no man than this, that a man*
> *lay down his life for his friends.*
>
> JOHN 15:13 KJV

I was headed to Professor Conrad's English class with less than excitement. As usual, he would drone his way through the lecture with little or no emotion. His iron gray hair, blue eyes, and craggy face only emphasized the boring way he expressed himself. During class a student asked a question that allowed Professor Conrad to talk about love. "When you really love someone you give everything," he said. "There's no 50 percent or 75 percent in love. You give 100 percent. There's no measurement in the giving or receiving in unconditional love." Then he started to talk about his wife and how much he loved her. His eyes twinkled and his voice was tender. It was not only what he was saying but how he was saying it that changed my heart that day. Instantly I saw Professor Conrad in a new light.

God spoke to me about love through this most unusual source, and suddenly my heart was changed forever. I had read about love in 1 Corinthians 13, but after hearing those words, I began to understand what love really is. Through years of marriage, children, and grandchildren, as I changed a diaper, tucked a little one in bed, or prepared a meal when I was almost too weary to stand, the words "unconditional love" echoed in my heart and a smile began to weave across my face.

LIVE ON PURPOSE

Agape love, or unconditional love, only comes from God. It's the kind of love that gives 100 percent—the kind of love that lays down its life for another. God is the only One who can develop it in you, because the natural man does not understand it. John 13:35 says that the world will know you are Christians by your love.

First Corinthians 13 says that even the greatest achievements are nothing without love. Check your motivations. If you are lacking in the area of love, ask God to help you develop this most important gift.

PRAYER

Father God, I want to know Your love better.
I want to walk in that love on a regular basis.
Teach me more about it. Show me how to act in love.
Help me to love others, in Jesus' name.

The Peace of God

KEN

> And the peace of God, which passeth all understanding,
> shall keep your hearts and minds through Christ Jesus.
>
> PHILIPPIANS 4:7 KJV

I've always endeavored to keep the peace of God in my heart regarding decisions. Well, I thought I would never go to Bible school, but one day while reading a Christian magazine I saw an ad for a school led by a leader I greatly respect. I thought if I did go, this school would be the one. I couldn't get away from thinking about that school. I had such peace in my heart about going, so I finally did it. Those years changed my life forever. My spiritual walk was greatly increased and I met people that helped develop my character and my gifts.

While in Bible school, I met a girl who loved God like I did and had a desire to minister to others. Three years after graduating, we were both still in the same town where we went to school. Every time I thought of her, there was that peace in my heart again. I knew in my spirit that she would honor me as much as I would honor her. We have been married now for eight years and have three awesome children. We moved to a new area to pastor a church, and my wife has been right there to help me. I was highly blessed to follow the peace in my heart concerning these very important decisions. The peace of God is down deep inside of you. There is a green light (not a red one) that says it's okay to proceed through if you have the right of way.

LIVE ON PURPOSE

The enemy cannot imitate the peace of God. That's why God often leads you by peace. Sometimes the Lord sends a supernatural sign, but most of the time He will lead you by peace. Make it a point in your life to ask God about your decisions, and then wait to see how that decision sits with your inner man.

PRAYER

Father God, thank You that You lead me by Your peace and that Your peace guards my heart and mind. I commit myself to check in with You when I am making decisions. I welcome Your leadership in my life, in Jesus' name.

Every Opportunity

PAULA

> *Be very careful, then, how you live–not as unwise*
> *but as wise, making the most of every opportunity,*
> *because the days are evil. Therefore do not be foolish,*
> *but understand what the Lord's will is.*
>
> EPHESIANS 5:15-17 NIV

"I got it!" I shouted. I had just received news that I was awarded a scholarship for full tuition to the college near our home. God made a way for me to go to college, and now it was up to me to do my part. The first day of finding my classes and getting my books was a whirl of activities. In a few days, classes became routine and meeting new friends was a bonus. I was elected secretary of the honor society, and even met my husband during my years at college.

Many times throughout my life, God has opened doors just like the one He opened for me to attend college.

Each time I had to do my part, and each time He faithfully saw me through to success.

LIVE ON PURPOSE

James 1:17 says that every good and perfect
gift comes from God. If it's good, it's God.
So don't waste any opportunities that God
gives you. If you have, then ask for
forgiveness and for a new opportunity.
God's got lots of them for you.

PRAYER

*Father God, help me to make the most of every
opportunity. I want to understand what Your will
is every day. And help me to enjoy the good things
that You are doing for me all the time, in Jesus' name.*

His Witness

W. E.

The fruit of the righteous is a tree of life,
And he who wins souls is wise.

PROVERBS 11:30 NKJV

One day while I was working on a piece of equipment in the shop, a salesman drove into the driveway. I heard the Lord speak to my heart, *This man is hurting.*

Ron, the salesman, was selling shop supplies and I had plenty.

Inside, I heard the Lord again, *If you don't buy something, how will you tell him about Me?*

So I bought some hacksaw blades and welding rods. Then I felt like I should just ask him about Jesus. "Ron, have you ever asked the Lord into your life?"

He replied, "No."

"Would you like to ask Him now?"

He said, "Yes." I reached for a little Gideon Bible I kept in my toolbox. We said the sinner's prayer written in the back together.

Ron replied, "I have been reading this Bible all winter and it never made any sense to me, but you made it so plain."

Of course, it wasn't me; it was the Holy Spirit that helped him understand.

LIVE ON PURPOSE

Have you ever felt the Lord was leading you to share about your faith? Did you? Sometimes we may feel uncomfortable approaching someone about what they believe, but when the Lord leads you to do so, He is giving you an opportunity to be part of that person's salvation. Even if you are rejected, you are still planting a seed in that person's life that will turn them to Jesus. And many times, that person may be ready to accept Jesus right there. Will you be His witness?

PRAYER

Lord, thank You that I hear Your voice. When You have an opportunity for me to be a witness, help me to be bold and give me the words to say. I refuse to fear what others may think of me. When I am doing Your will, I know that I am doing exactly what I should be, in Jesus' name.

Humble

ELIZABETH

> *So humble yourselves under the mighty power of God, and*
> *in his good time he will honor you. Give all your worries*
> *and cares to God, for he cares about what happens to you.*
>
> 1 PETER 5:6,7 NLT

I felt a release from God to quit a job where I was treated poorly. I applied at several places and even got a job, but I just could not take it. I had no peace. I fasted. I prayed. I talked to my pastors. They encouraged me to continue to seek the Lord in prayer, and they spent several mornings praying with me. Finally one Saturday night I was desperate to hear from God. I was running out of money and I needed to take a job or move. So I confessed every Scripture promise I could find. I prayed in the spirit. Then I began to worship God and dance before Him. When I was exhausted, I became still before the Lord. In my spirit I saw the Lord break through the dark clouds. His light was so bright that it washed away the darkness. Light was streaming everywhere. He said to me, *Well done. I want you to move to Tulsa.* I had it in my heart at that time to move to Tulsa, but I had no direction from God until then to make the move. I packed my entire apartment that night and finished up just in time to get ready for church on Sunday morning. I went to lunch that day with my pastors and told them what happened. They must have had peace about it as well, because they helped me pack my truck. I left for Tulsa the following day. Within two weeks, I had a great new job in Tulsa.

LIVE ON PURPOSE

When you don't know what to do, humble yourself before the Lord. When you come to God, He will answer you. Elizabeth humbled herself before the Lord, but her answer did not come immediately. She did all she knew to do, and then she waited on God and her answer came. If you are anxious or worried about a situation, humble yourself before God. Cast your cares on Him, and then wait for Him to give you the answer.

PRAYER

Father God, in Jesus' name, I give to You my cares. I humble myself before You, realizing that my answer needs to come from You. Show me what I should do and help me to carry it out.

Sustained by God

ANGEL

> *Cast your cares on the Lord and he will sustain you;*
> *he will never let the righteous fall.*
>
> PSALM 55:22 NIV

I was in Moscow with a sore throat and fever. My job required that I take a trip overseas to help edit a book project. I stayed with a pastor's family and attended church services when I wasn't working. By the middle of the trip, I was feeling very ill. Not able to go to a Russian hospital, I had to draw on the power of God to pull me through the rigorous schedule. One night, God woke me up and said, *Let it all go.* Not only was I sick, God wanted to deal with my heart! Desperate for relief in my throat and soul, I let go by faith. I found out that God only needed my permission to take the pain, bitterness, and unforgiveness that were clogging my soul. That trip ended with a job completed and a changed heart. But I still had a sore throat! I got back to the States and had opportunities open up immediately to minister in several states. About a month after my trip to Russia, I finally ended up at the doctor's office. He diagnosed a severe case of strep throat. God's power had sustained me overseas *and* at home, giving me the supernatural ability to minister in ways I had never experienced before! I now know that I can access God's anointing wherever I am by letting go of my abilities and problems and letting God take over.

LIVE ON PURPOSE

Is there an area of your life where you are struggling? Are you holding on to the cares of life instead of giving them to God? He's ready to help you, but He needs your permission to move. Check your life today. What area do you need to turn over to God?

PRAYER

Lord, I do not want to hold on to cares, bitterness, or unforgiveness. I turn these things over to You now. Show me if there are areas where I need to make changes, in Jesus' name.

Living Letter

SUSAN

You show and make obvious that you are a letter from Christ delivered by us, not written with ink but with [the] Spirit of [the] living God, not on tablets of stone but on tablets of human hearts.

2 CORINTHIANS 3:3 AMP

I was working in a custom photo lab where the staff was very young and inexperienced. It was chaotic and I wasn't sure why God had me there. I did my best to be a light in that dark place, but I felt like many times my witness backfired. My life was so different, in a way, it caused me to be ostracized from the other associates. There were a couple of other Christians in the company, but they worked in another area and I did not see them much. Eventually God led me to leave that company and move to another state. Before I left, one of the top salespeople came to me and asked me some questions about being a Christian. She told me that I was the first sold-out

Christian she had ever met that was normal. It made me see that God had used my life as a light to her, even though I couldn't tell until I was ready to leave.

LIVE ON PURPOSE

You are God's light in the earth. He works through you to reach others. Even though you may not think anyone is looking at your life or even that anyone cares, God ministers to others through your example. Be encouraged and continue to be a light to others. You may never know the difference you made while you are here on the earth, but God knows and He rewards those who seek Him. (Heb. 11:6.)

PRAYER

Lord, help me to be a light in my world. I don't always feel like I'm perfect, but I know that You can minister to others through me. I open myself up to whatever You want to do. Help me to help others, in Jesus' name.

Acknowledgments

Harrison House would like to thank the following
people for the life experiences they contributed to this work:

Aaron Whisner

Abraham Sarker

Ali Roe

Alice James

Alyssa Whisner

Amanda Moringo

Amy Sarker

Angel Ausdemore

April Meyers

Billy Cleary

Brittany Sawyer

Caleb Cross

Christopher Janos

Clifford Moore

Devon Davoux

Diana Erwin

Elizabeth Janos

Erik Jackson

Gary Cole

Hanna Jackson

Jayne Sleeter

Jonathan D. Coon

Joshua Childs

Julie Lechlider

Julie Werner

Kate Paulsen

Ken Semeschuk

Kyle Loffelmacher

Lauren Hagvewood

Lizzy Janos

Marcine Tiahrt

Mike Benton

Natalie Jackson

Patrick Loder

Paula Bednarek

Rebecka Eliasson

Renoulte Allen

Robin Loder

Sarah Wehrli

Sheila Small

Tim Burton

Tracie Hunsberger

Trecie Williams

W. E. Tiahrt

Prayer of Salvation

God loves you—no matter who you are, no matter what your past. God loves you so much that He gave His one and only begotten Son for you. The Bible tells us that "...whoever believes in him shall not perish but have eternal life" (John 3:16 NIV). Jesus laid down His life and rose again so that we could spend eternity with Him in heaven and experience His absolute best on earth. If you would like to receive Jesus into your life, say the following prayer out loud and mean it from your heart.

Heavenly Father, I come to You admitting that I am a sinner. Right now, I choose to turn away from sin, and I ask You to cleanse me of all unrighteousness. I believe that Your Son, Jesus, died on the cross to take away my sins. I also believe that He rose again from the dead so that I might be forgiven of my sins and made righteous through faith in Him. I call upon the name of Jesus Christ to be the Savior and Lord of my life. Jesus, I choose to follow You and ask that You fill me with the power of the Holy Spirit. I declare that right now I am a child of God. I am free from sin and full of the righteousness of God. I am saved in Jesus' name. Amen.

If you prayed this prayer to receive Jesus Christ as your Savior for the first time, please contact us on the Web at **www.harrisonhouse.com** to receive a free book.

Or you may write to us at:
Harrison House
P.O. Box 35035
Tulsa, Oklahoma 74153

*Please include your prayer requests
and comments when you write.*

Live the Life You Were Born to Live

Destiny is built on thousands of moments—opportunities to seek God's will, to seek His direction in the experience of every day. Let the *Life on Purpose Series* encourage you to make the most of every moment.

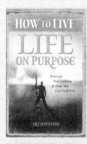

How to Live Life on Purpose™
ISBN 1-57794-321-X

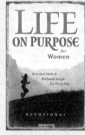

Life on Purpose™ *for Women*
ISBN 1-57794-649-9

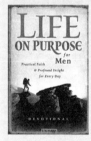

Life on Purpose™ *for Men*
ISBN 1-57794-648-0

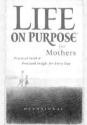

Life on Purpose™ *for Mothers*
ISBN 1-57794-683-9

Available at fine bookstores everywhere
or visit www.harrisonhouse.com.

PRAY WITH POWER

Prayers That Avail Much for Graduates
1-57794-664-8

With school behind you and a mountain of decision and responsibilities ahead of you, you need the strength of God's Word to see you through. *Prayers That Avail Much® for Graduates* makes it easier than ever to tap into God's wisdom through prayers based on His Word. You can pray with confidence knowing you are praying what God has already promised for you in His Word.

Prayers include:

- God's Wisdom and His Will

- Finances

- Finding Favor With Others

- Equipped for Success

- Your Future Spouse

- To Live Free From Worry

- When You Feel Lonely

- And More!

Available at bookstore everywhere
or visit www.harrisonhouse.com.

when it's time to move on

1. find your life's quest

2. find your place to belong

3. find friends for life

4. bartel—the Oneighy guy. over twenty years of congratulating graduates. over twenty years of counseling graduates. now you can find the answers.

little black book
for
graduates

by blaine bartel

Little Black Book for Graduates
1-57794-612-X

THE FUTURE IS YOURS.

Load Up Pocket Devotional
1-57794-651-0

What you do with your life determines the future. You are only one person, but God can take one person and change nations. In the prophetic age that we live, He is looking for nation changers. That may sound unreal, but with God it is absolutely possible. These 31 devotions can revolutionize your future. Get to know God and take hold of your future.

www.harrisonhouse.com

Fast. Easy. Convenient!

◆ New Book Information
◆ Look Inside the Book
◆ Press Releases
◆ Bestsellers

◆ Free E-News
◆ Author Biographies
◆ Upcoming Books
◆ Share Your Testimony

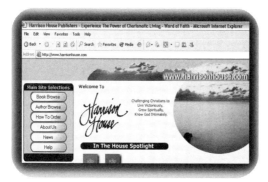

For the latest in book news and author information, please visit us on the Web at www.harrisonhouse.com. Get up-to-date pictures and details on all our powerful and life-changing products. Sign up for our e-mail newsletter, *Friends of the House,* and receive free monthly information on our authors and products including testimonials, author announcements, and more!

Harrison House—
Books That Bring Hope, Books That Bring Change

The Harrison House Vision

Proclaiming the truth and the power

Of the Gospel of Jesus Christ

With excellence;

Challenging Christians to

Live victoriously,

Grow spiritually,

Know God intimately.